D1830838

INDIA AND THE INDIAN OCEAN

Owing to the antiquity and rarity of this book, certain pages are regrettably absent, and readability is compromised due to the blurring of the original text. If you possess any insights regarding the availability of these missing sections, kindly inform us. Your assistance is crucial in ensuring the completion of this significant work for the benefit of future generations.

INDIA AND THE INDIAN OCEAN

An Essay on the Influence of Sea Power on Indian History

BY

K. M. Panikkar

GYAN

Published by

GYAN

Gyan Publishing House
5, Ansari Road
Daryaganj, New Delhi-110002
Phone: 011-47034999, 9811692060
E-mail: books@gyanbooks.com

Distribution Network
gyanbooks.com
India, USA, Canada, UK, Australia

© Publisher

All rights reserved. No part of this work may be reproduced, stored, adapted, or transmitted in any form or by any means, electronic, mechanical, photocopying, micro-filming, recording or otherwise, or translated in any language, without the prior written permission of the copyright owner and the publisher.

ISBN: 978-81-212-5547-9 (HB)
First Published, 1945

2nd Impression 2024

Printed at: Gyan Press, Delhi.

The book is sold subject to the condition that it shall not, by way of trade or otherwise, be lent, resold, hired out, or otherwise circulated without the prior publisher's written consent.

INDIA AND THE INDIAN OCEAN
Author: K. M. PANIKKAR

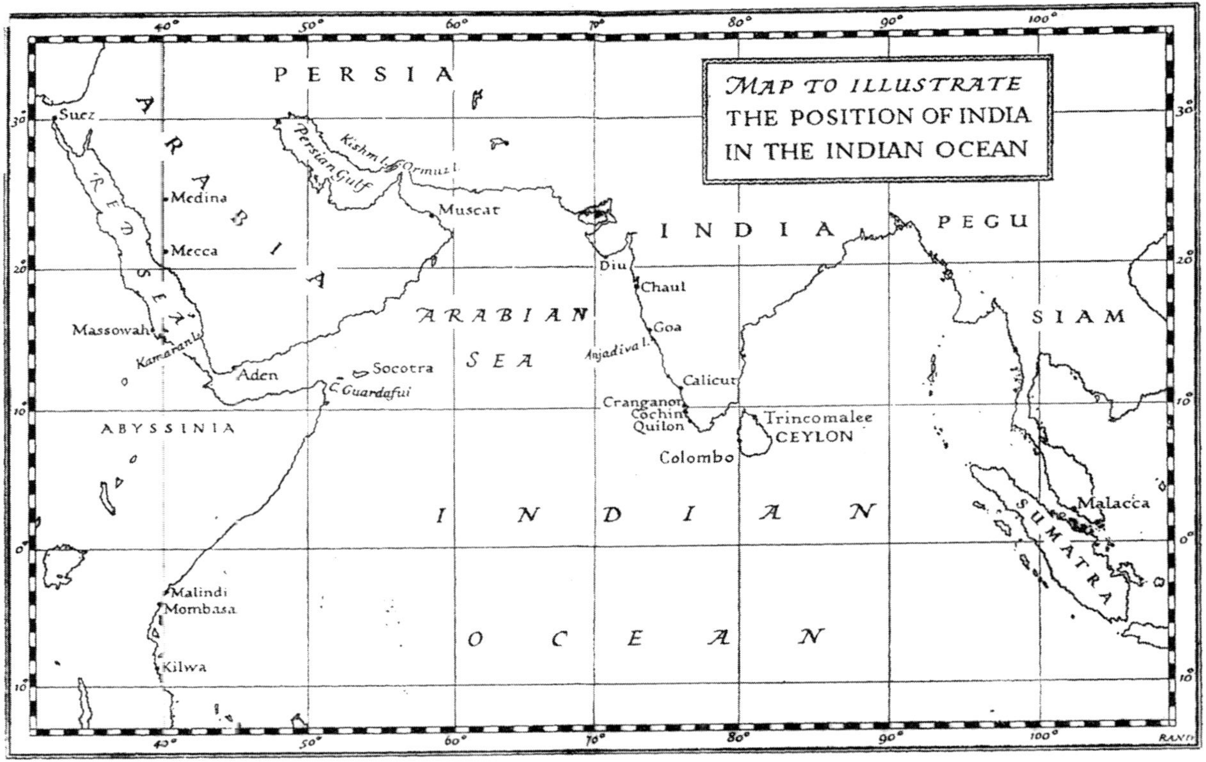
MAP TO ILLUSTRATE
THE POSITION OF INDIA
IN THE INDIAN OCEAN
PERSIA
ARABIA
Suez
Medina
Mecca
RED SEA
Massowah
Kamaran I.
Aden
Persian Gulf
Kishm I.
Ormuz I.
Muscat
Socotra
C. Guardafui
ABYSSINIA
ARABIAN
SEA
INDIA
Diu
Chaul
Goa
Anjadiva I.
Calicut
Cranganor
Cochin
Quilon
Colombo
Trincomalee
CEYLON
PEGU
SIAM
Malacca
SUMATRA
INDIAN
OCEAN
Malindi
Mombasa
Kilwa
40°
50°
60°
70°
80°
90°
100°
30°
20°
10°
0°
10°

INDIA AND THE INDIAN OCEAN

INDIA AND THE INDIAN OCEAN

An Essay on the influence of Sea Power on Indian History

by

K. M. PANIKKAR

London

GEORGE ALLEN & UNWIN LTD

Contents

Introduction

"He who rules on the sea will shortly rule on the land also" declared Khaireddin Barbarosa to Sultan Suleiman the Magnificent. The history of no country illustrates this principle better than that of India. There have been invasions and conquests of India from the land side on many previous occasions. But such invasions and conquests have either led to transient political changes, or to the foundation of new dynasties, which in a very short time became national and Indian. In fact it may truly be said that India never lost her independence till she lost the command of the sea in the first decade of the sixteenth century.

In the following pages an attempt is made to trace the influence of the Indian Ocean on the shaping of Indian history and to discuss the vital importance of oceanic control to the future of India. There has been an unfortunate tendency to overlook the sea in the discussion of India's defence problems Until now, the discussion has proceeded on the assumption that the security of India is a matter exclusively of the North-West Frontier and of a strong enough army to resist any aggression across the Hindu Kush. This is an entirely one-sided view of Indian history. No doubt most of the invasions of India have come from that side; and others may come from that quarter in the future also. The North-West Frontier and perhaps the North-East Frontier also will therefore remain important strategic areas for the defence of India. But an examination of the factors of Indian defence will show that ever since the sixteenth century from which time the Indian Ocean became the scene of a struggle for the control of the sea, the future of India has been determined not on the land frontiers, but on the oceanic expanse which washes the three sides of India.

It is true that till the beginning of the sixteenth century Oceanic problems had not intruded themselves on the history of the mainland. The reasons for this are obvious. In the first place, the control of the Indian waters was in Indian hands till the middle of the thirteenth century, and no power strong enough to challenge Indian control appeared on the ocean. The Arabs who succeeded to the supremacy of the sea, after the breakdown of Chola naval power were only commercial navigators and were not the instruments of any national policy, nor had they the support of any organised government. In short till the arrival of the Portuguese at Calicut, *no naval power* had appeared on Indian waters.

What Vasco da Gama and his successors introduced into Indian history was the claim to an exclusive control of the seas, a conception wholly at variance with what had been accepted as the " natural law " both in Europe and in Asia. The might of Portugal was organised in order to enforce such a claim, and Alfonso Albuquerque by conquering Socotra, Ormuz and Malacca and by organising an impregnable territorial base in India established effectively that supremacy of the sea which his master claimed on the basis of the Bull of Pope Calixtus III. From that time till today the Ocean has dominated India. The unique glory of the Moghuls could not hide the fact that on the sea they were totally helpless, and Akbar himself had to suffer the humiliation of the trade of the Empire being interrupted and the pilgrim traffic to Mecca harassed by the Portuguese on his coast. The Moghuls with their Central Asian tradition had no recognition of the importance of the sea. It is only when the Sidis of Janjira offered their services against the growing Maratha power on the sea that Aurangazib gave his half-hearted recognition to a fleet being organised on a reasonable scale. On the whole, the Moghul view of the sea was that of Kalif Omar who when he was told by his General, at the time of the conquest of Egypt, that *"the sea was a huge beast which silly folk ride like worms on logs " ordered that no Mussalman should risk his life on such an unruly element without his express orders. The result was that during the 200 years of Moghul greatness, not only was the Indian sea entirely under alien control but

* Stanley Lane Poole, *Barbary Corsairs*, p. 7.

simultaneously with the development of Moghul power, the foundation was being laid by others for a more complete subjection of India, than any land power at any time could have conceived.

The importance of the sea came to be recognised by the Indian Rulers only when it was too late. Sivaji was near enough to the Portuguese base of Goa to realise its importance and did initiate a policy of naval expansion which in the heyday of Maratha power ruled the Konkan waters. Hyder Ali also did not fail to realise its vital importance as his agreement with the Bailee de Suffren conclusively proves. But by the time of Sivaji the control of the seas had already passed to to the Dutch and the British; and by the time of Hyder Ali, the British were the undoubted masters of the Indian Ocean, though the transcendent genius of Suffren eclipsed the fact for a short time.

For 157 years (i.e. since the departure of Suffren in 1784 to the fall of Singapore in 1941) the mastery of the sea over Indian history was complete but unobtrusive. The question of sea power did not arise as the Indian Ocean was a British lake. It was as natural and as normal as the air we breathed. during that time and no one was interested in discovering the relation of the sea to Indian Defence. In the result the entire emphasis was on the land frontier and Indian Defence was equated with the maintenance of a powerful army on the North-West Frontier.

The rivalry of world navies which, in the interlude between the two great wars, became so important a factor in international politics made Great Britain recognise the importance of regional navies. A Royal Indian Navy was therefore created, more as a symbol and a beginning than as a fighting arm, for the question of any one seriously challenging British supremacy in the Indian Ocean could not then be conceived. If such a challenge materialised it could only be as a result of a breakdown of Britain's naval strength and in that contingency any naval force that could be created in India would hardly be of serious use for the defence of India. The immediate object of the Royal Indian Navy was therefore no more than the establishment of a force in India which would take over coastal duties and at the same time create a naval tradition in the country.

A beginning was indeed made, but the conditions under which the Indian Navy had to develop may best be realised from the following summary of a speech by Admiral Fitzherbert:

> *"The outlook when he first arrived in India was heartbreaking. Not the slightest attention was paid to the sea by the authorities, and he likened himself to Christian in the *Pilgrim's Progress* when he found the powers of darkness arrayed as a solid phalanx in front of him and between him and his desires, which were to teach India how vital the sea was to her and how much she needed a modern fighting Navy.
>
> " He started off on a very ' sticky wicket ': he was informed by the India Office that India was bankrupt; the defence budget was too small, and was concentrated on the military side to the exclusion of the Navy and the Air Force, and he had to fight alone. He started from the beginning and gradually worked ahead; he got some funds and the Chatfield Commission did a great deal to help him. The Navy consisted only of five little ships, two of which were converted yachts. When he left there were ninety modern ships. He started with 1,200 officers and men; when he left India there were 23,000. He would like to correct General Molesworth, because the Royal Indian Navy had expanded by 1,800 per cent. . . . The expansion of the Royal Indian Navy was rapid and fairly large, and one of his chief troubles was the difficulty of training. Schools could be built, recruits could be enlisted, but trained instructors could not be produced for such a large expansion, but his instructional staff had achieved the impossible; they were magnificent. Although they all wanted to get to sea to fight the enemy

* *Asiatic Review*, January, 1944, pp. 8 and 9.

they stayed in the schools and did their job so well that they were able to keep pace with the training requirements. He could not put into words what he owed to his training staff.

"With regard to the expansion of ships, he produced a construction programme by means of which every shipbuilding slip in India was filled; when a ship slipped down into the sea the keel was laid for the next. He had very great co-operation from shipbuilding experts and others who overcame all difficulties. The problems were new, but they shouldered the burden, and he was very grateful to them all. Ships were built in India, Australia, the United Kingdom and the United States, and gradually they came into service, and when the plan was complete there would be not 5, but 250 modern ships in the Royal Indian Navy. Recruits were being enlisted at the rate of 1,000 a month, so that his 23,000 would now be nearing the 30,000 mark. Two major naval bases had been built and three minor bases fitted with the needs of a modern minor naval base, so that attention had not only been given to ships and men, but to the housing problem.

"A modern navy needed a large number of very technical training schools. When he left he was happy in the knowledge that India's Navy possessed every type of technical training school needed for a fighting navy, which were producing the trained men and officers required.

"Referring to the efforts of the Royal Indian Navy at sea, Admiral Fitzherbert said that the ships had been employed in fighting or helping to fight the battle of the Atlantic and had operated as far east as Singapore and as far south as Australia; they had come up against the enemy, the enemy mine and the enemy gun, and they had done magnificently. The men had had their ships sunk under them, and in every case their behaviour had accorded with the very highest traditions of the Imperial Navy in times of great stress and hardship."

What the Royal Indian Navy has achieved during this War is indeed a glorious page in Indian history. It is noteworthy that in the naval action which led to the landing of troops in Iran, it was an Indian officer from Calicut, that great centre of naval activity in the past, that boarded the Persian Admiral's sloop and shot him.

A naval power however well organised from the point of view of warships and fighting personnel cannot count for much in the sea unless it is supplemented by a great national mercantile marine. The nineteenth century witnessed the disappearance of Indian-built ships from the high seas. Mercantile shipping on the Indian waters including coastal waters was monopolised by foreign interests. The complete lack of attention to the sea by the authorities, which Admiral Fitzherbert emphasised, was never more clearly seen than in the hostility in the early stages and the indifference in the later stages to Indian shipping displayed by landsmen in Delhi and Simla. To them the attempt of Indians to create a national mercantile marine seemed at best a wastage of effort when the British Companies were there to provide the services more efficiently and perhaps at less cost. The European interests in India looked upon it as an outstanding example of anti-British feeling and a manifestation of racial hostility. The fight of Scindia Steam Navigation Company for a share in the sea traffic of the Indian Ocean and the Bay of Bengal is indeed only the counterpart of Admiral Fitzherbert's fight in the interests of the Royal Indian Navy. India owes a deep debt of gratitude to Narottam Morarji who in spite of almost insuperable difficulties developed an Indian mercantile marine and to Admiral Fitzherbert who in the face of the odds against him transformed a navy of five small vessels in the short period of 5 years into a fighting arm of 250 warships able to carry the Indian flag into distant waters.

What is the true function of naval power in regard to land defence, especially in relation to India? In the heyday of British supremacy of the seas Admiral Mahan drew attention to the dominating role that sea power has played in shaping the course of world history. It is perhaps just to remember that Mahan's view was biased by the unique authority of Britain, an island power basing its dominion in all parts of the world on the supremacy of the seas. Today the pendulum has swung in the opposite direction. Hilaire Belloc, representing the continental military tradition does not hesitate to say :

The failure of efforts made by sea*"is an illustration of something which you find running all through military history, to wit, the dependence of sea power in military affairs is a lure leading to ultimate disappointment. In the final and decisive main duels of history the party which begins with high sea power is defeated by the land power; whether that sea power be called Carthage, or Athens, or the Phoenician fleet of the Great King, it loses in the long run and the land power wins."

The land strategists have generally held this view. Even Mackinder who thought of the world as an island emphasising that sea power depended on land bases points out †"Hannibal struck overland at the Peninsular base of Roman seapower and that base was saved by victory on land . . . So impressive have been the results of British sea power that there has perhaps been a tendency to neglect the warnings of history and to regard sea power in general as inevitably having, because of the unity of the Ocean, the last word in the rivalry with land power."

It is obvious that sea power can only conquer the sea and hold the sea; only the army can conquer or hold the land. But the advantage that a naval power has against countries whose main line of communications lie on the sea are obvious. Even against a dominant land power supremacy of the sea has undoubted advantages. It can land at any point of its choice, reinforce its troops, transport large masses of men continuously without fatigue and feint at distant points. True, once the landing is effected, it is the land power that counts; but even then the importance of sea power in safe-

* *The Crusades*, p. 68.

† *Democratic Ideals and Realities*.

guarding the communication and in carrying out an effective withdrawal cannot be overestimated. The fate of Alexander's marauding host after his raid on India would have undoubtedly been the same as that of Napoleon's Grand Army but for the Greek Admiral Nearchus' ability to transport the troops on Indian-built vessels over the sea. From that time to Dunkirk this position has been established on a hundred battle fields.

So far as India is concerned, it should be remembered that the peninsular character of the country and the essential dependence of its trade on maritime traffic give the sea a preponderant influence on its destiny. Though a conquest from the side of the sea against an established land power is not a possibility, especially when we consider that it was only *after* the breakdown of the Moghul Empire that such a conquest was ever attempted and that it also took no less than 100 years (from the siege of Arcot to the defeat of the Sikhs) to complete—the fact can never be overlooked that the economic life of India will be completely at the mercy of the power which controls the seas. Also the security of India could be perpetually threatened, for it is but seldom that fortified land posts held under the cover of naval guns by a power having the command of the seas have been successfully attacked from the land side. All the efforts of the Moghuls did not succeed in reducing the small settlements which were defended from the sea. The successive efforts of Spanish armies have not been able to reduce Gibraltar and if Singapore fell to a land attack, it was only because the command of the sea had been lost for the time. With the open coastline of over 2,000 miles, there will clearly be no safety for India, if the Indian Ocean ceases to be a protected sea.

British authority in India hangs on the thin thread of safe naval communications. Till 1941 that thread seemed strong enough. But if the Indian Ocean became once again a theatre of naval rivalry, India will be no more safe than China was for a hundred years, when it was the cockpit of European ambitions, or is today when it is under the iron heel of a naval power strong enough to control the coastal seas.

But can the Indian Ocean become once again a protected area, a reserved sphere of Anglo-Indian influence, especially when America is well established in the Pacific and other powerful nations may make their appearance on the eastern waters? The doctrine of "the indivisibility of the sea" which Admiral Mahan emphasised so greatly may perhaps lead us to think that if America establishes her unchallenged mastery in the southern and middle Pacific, her power is bound to be felt as much in the Indian Ocean as in other areas of the Oceanic surface. But the indivisible sea is no longer indivisible. Air power has introduced a new factor in the control of seas. It can extend across the waters and its possession gives to land powers a weapon whose range and effectiveness will necessitate a revision of strategic locations. With mastery of the air it becomes easier to control the territorially vital seas and oceanic space values have therefore to be considered in the broadest terms. If a steel ring can be created around India with their air and naval bases at suitable points and if within the area so ringed, a navy can be created strong enough to defend its homewaters, then the waters vital to India's security and prosperity can be protected and converted into an area of safety. With the islands of the Bay of Bengal with Singapore, Mauritius and Socotra, properly equipped and protected and with a navy based on Ceylon security can return to that part of the Indian Ocean which is of supreme importance to India.

It need hardly be said that such an Oceanic policy for India is possible only in the closest collaboration and association with Britain. An independent India, cannot for at least half a century or even more undertake so great a responsibility. Even if she were in a position to do so, which she obviously is not, Great Britain's own interests in the Ocean are such that it will be nothing short of national suicide for her to withdraw from that area. Therefore no less in Indian than in British interests, the defence of the Indian Ocean must be a joint effort of India and Britain. It is for Britain and India to devise a machinery by which this aim can be effectively fulfilled.

I have tried to examine in the chapters that follow not only the part that India has played in the past in the navigation and control of the Oceanic area, and the effects of the control of the Indian seas by European nations, but the problems likely to arise in the future if British naval supremacy is challenged by any power in this area. The future of India will undoubtedly be decided on the sea. It is indissolubly connected with developments in the Indian Ocean. India cannot therefore afford to take the selfish view that the control of the sea is Britain's job and that our freedom will be allowed to grow and develop within a protected magic circle.

Our vision has been obscured by an un-Indian wave of pacificism. *Ahimsa* is no doubt a great religious creed, but that is a creed which India rejected when she refused to follow Gautama Buddha. The Hindu theory at all times, especially in the periods of her historic greatness was one of active assertion of the right, if necessary through the force of arms. It is not for *Ahimsa* and pacificism that Ramchandra stands in Indian religion; it is for an active assertion of what is morally right. Nor does Krishna stand for non-violence. "Wake, be thyself, scourge thy foes" is the manly teaching of the Gita. Apart from the Buddhist and Jain heresies which the good sense of the Hindus rejected long ago, it is not known what religious basis there is in Hinduism for the form of pacificism which has come, for some strange reason, to be associated with the Hindus. Once we are free from the effects of this idea, and are thus enabled to look facts in the face, it will be clear that Indian freedom can be achieved and upheld only by firmly deciding to shoulder our share at all costs in the active defence of the areas necessary for our security. To the Indian Ocean we shall then have to turn, as our ancestors did, who conquered Socotra long before the Christian Era and established an Empire in the Pacific which lasted for 1500 years.

CHAPTER I

INDIAN OCEAN

The importance of geographical facts on the development of history is only now receiving wide and general recognition. Geopolitics as a handmaid of warfare and as a guide for political programmes may be a recent psuedo science, but as early as the fourth century B.C. we have in Kautalya a definition of *chakravartipatha*, boundaries and lands which should belong to any empire. " The territory (of the Empire), he defines, " is the earth : viz. the area between the Himalayas and the sea which is 9,000 Yojanas in extent running northward obliquely." The essential importance of the factors of geography as conditioning the growth of nations and States was never in dispute, though its actual formulation as a science and consequent elaboration in its different aspects is a recent development.

Even in respect of the modern science of Geopolitics, India can claim to be a pioneer. The question of suitable land frontiers agitated the great minds of Anglo-India from the time of Warren Hastings; Malcolm, Metcalfe, Elphinstone and others were no mean students of the problem. But it was Lord Curzon who gave to the question of frontiers a scientific basis and emphasised its importance as a subject worthy of serious study. Durand, Holditch and Younghusband were protagonists of a regular theory of geopolitics. But they were essentially landsmen. Lord Curzon himself thought of the sea only as a *frontier* and not as a vital territorial area. In a noble passage he elaborates his views as follows : "It was because of the interposition of the sea that England lost America ; that the Dutch and the Portuguese lost the greater part of their Indian Empires, that Napoleon equally with Rome experienced so many difficulties in Egypt, that the Mexican adventure of France and Austria ended in a fiasco, that Spain was robbed almost in a day of her possessions in

Cuba, Puerto Rico and the Phillippines." The Indian Ocean naturally did not interest him and his school. This lack of interest in oceanic problems was such that India willingly agreed to part with the administration of Aden, one of the key points for the control of the Oceanic area.

If interest in the problems of the Indian Ocean was absent in India itself, it is not a matter of surprise that it did not receive much attention from the writers on Geopolitics elsewhere. The German thinkers who have devoted most attention to the examination of geographical problems have been obsessed with the question of Nazi world strategy in pursuit of the view that the control of land, sea and air must ultimately pass to the power which controlled the pivotal land area in Europe. Mackinder who can legitimately claim to be the founder of the new school, thought equally in terms of the Eurasian continent and consequently the Indian Ocean was considered only as a link area of " The World Island " of which the only effective political boundaries were the Atlantic and the Pacific. In the result the problem of spatial dynamics in the Indian Ocean has not been intensively studied. The Pacific on the other hand was surveyed with meticulous care by Haushofer in his Geo Politik of the Pacific Ocean, a virtual text book for Nippon's naval strategy. The Atlantic has also been the subject of much specialised work. The fact that during the last 100 years preceding the Pacific War the Indian Ocean was a closed area from which international rivalries were excluded was perhaps one of the reasons which contributed to this neglect. Further, from the point of view of power politics the areas bordering on the Indian Ocean did not count in the period before the War.

This neglect can no longer be justified. The waters of the world form one vast expanse. While land may be enveloped by the sea—and the Continents are so enveloped—the Oceans are divided only by artificial boundaries. Admiral Mahan the prophet of the indivisible sea took as his text the quotation from Genesis " And God said, let the waters be gathered together in one place." The oneness of the sea is an obvious geographical fact, though as we shall see later scientific inventions have made it possible to bring large areas of oceanic surface under the control of land powers and thus to convert them into closed seas. From this point of view the geographical structure of the Indian Ocean is particularly important. For the most part its area is walled off on three sides by land, with the southern side of Asia forming a roof over it. The continent of Africa constitutes the western wall, while Burma, Malaya and the insular continuations protect the eastern side. The vital feature which differentiates the Indian Ocean from the Pacific and the Atlantic is not the two sides but the sub-continent of India which juts out far into the sea for a thousand miles to its tapering end at Cape Comorin. It is the geographical position of India that changes the character of the Indian ocean.

Compared with the other oceans, this feature stands out most clearly. The Arctic and the Antarctic, circling the poles have but little connection with inhabited land. The Pacific and the Atlantic on the other hand lie from north to south like gigantic highways. They have no land roof, no vast land area jutting out into their expanse. Considered geographically the Indian Ocean in spite of the vastness of its surface and the oceanic character of its currents and winds is more like a land-locked sea.

Another important feature of this Ocean is the distribution of islands and archipelagoes near its continental shores or in its vastness. Apart from Ceylon which is attached geographically to India, and Madagascar which is near to the African mainland, the oceanic spaces do not possess the same distribution of islands which is so marked a feature of the Pacific. Even in the case of the Atlantic, Iceland, the Azores and the West Indian Archipelago, not to speak of Great Britain and Ireland, constitute a geographical feature of great importance.

The Indian Ocean washes the entire African east coast up to Somaliland, the South coast of Arabia, the Southern shores of Iran and Baluchistan, the peninsula of India, the western shores of Burma, the Malay Peninsula and Sumatra. Its eastern and western entrances are guarded by two narrow straits, the Bab el Mandeb and the Straits of Malacca both of which can be easily controlled From the Bab el Mandeb, the entrance is into the Red Sea, which being an inland sea is controlled by the lands on either side. The Straits of Malacca lead to the vast expanse of the Pacific, but here again the lands on either side become so narrow as to be easily capable of effective control of egress and ingress.

The main islands in the Ocean are Ceylon, which is so close to India as to lose its insular character, and Madagascar which by its size and position provides an ideal cover to the South-East coast of Africa. Ceylon has at least two fine harbours, Colombo and Trincomalee, whose importance has been recognised from time immemorial and Madagascar has unique facilities in Diego Suares which the Third Republic vainly converted into a base second only to Singapore in the Indian Ocean. The other islands of importance whose geographical situation has to be noticed are Socotra on the Arabian coast, Zanzibar and Seychelles on the East African side, Mauritius and Reunion on the tropic of Capricorn. The Laccadives and Maladives in the Arabian sea near the Indian coast, the Bahrein group near the Persian Gulf, the Andamans and the Nicobars in the Bay of Bengal and Penang are the other island features which have a great bearing on maritime history.

The distances have also to be kept in mind. The Andamans are over 800 miles from the nearest Indian port and over 400 miles from the Burmese side. Mauritius lies 2094 miles away from Colombo, while Socotra is no less than 1,000 miles. Penang is situated 1,278 miles away from Ceylon. The Laccadives and Maladives, small islets dotted over a great length to the South West of India provide no suitable harbour. In fact except Daman and Diu the Indian coast has no suitable islands near enough to afford cover.

The bays and bights of the Indian Ocean require special consideration. To the north-west corner is the Persian Gulf, a protected landlocked sea with Ormuz commanding the entry.

With the valley of the Euphrates and the Tigris and the historic land of Mesopotamia as its hinterland this sea has in the past had a dominant role in shaping the history of oceanic navigation and may in the future have even a greater influence than in the past.

The Arabian Sea, a vast expanse separating the two Peninsulas of India and Arabia and bounded on the north by the barren coast line of Persia is one of the vital seas of the world. As a result of the seasonal monsoon it has been for at least 3,000 years a great highway of commerce and intercourse. The Indians, the Phoenicians, the Arabs—in fact all the seafaring nations of the East—have considered this to be the chief area of navigation.

The Gulf of Aden is the bottleneck which is created by the projection of Africa and the South-eastern tip of Arabia, the two shores running more or less parallel here and ending at the straits of Bab el Mandeb. The entry to this Gulf from the east side is controlled by the island of Socotra. For ages it had been the home waters of the Arab corsairs who had their base in Aden a covered and almost hidden post on the coast of the tip of Arabia.

The Bay of Bengal, lying to the east of India and separating Burma and Malaya from the Peninsula of Hindustan is also governed by the monsoon. Further, it is said to be one of the four sea areas in the world subject to the phenomenon of revolving storms. From the ports on the East coast of India argosies have sailed this sea from the dawn of history and the colonisation of the Pacific islands by the Hindus shows the extent to which this sea had been explored and navigated at least 2,000 years ago.

The Gulf of Malacca is like the mouth of a crocodile, the Peninsula of Malaya being the upper and the jutting end of Sumatra being the lower jaw. The entry to the Gulf can be controlled by the Nicobars and the narrow end is dominated by the island of Malacca.

The wind currents of the area are specially important and are perhaps unique in the world in their effects. The monsoon whose regular action was discovered by Hippalus in A.D. 45 dominated the navigation of the Arabian sea and the Bay of Bengal till the invention of steamships in the nineteenth century. The South-west monsoon which blows across the Arabian sea determined for many thousand years the trade route which the ships followed. Following this wind they sailed from the Arabian and Red Sea ports to the coast of India Equally its flow into the Bay of Bengal and its return by the same route after a period of calm governed the sailing in that area also. Thus for a period of well over five months the direction and route of sailing were determined by these winds and the navigators of the Indian Ocean who had closely studied the action of these phenomena were able to make full use of it.

Allusion may also be made to the revolving storms of the Bay of Bengal, an ever present danger to shipping in that area. Another factor of importance relating to the Indian Ocean is its essentially tropical character. Its northern end does not go much beyond the Tropic of Cancer. Its land bounded area is therefore free from the effects of icebergs and other oceanic obstructions arising from the frozen polar regions. Heavy mists, fog and other difficulties which prevented early navigation are also absent in the Indian Ocean. The rigours of climate are also greatly modified by the geographic situation.

The lack of well defined " streams " like the Gulf Stream and its counterpart in the Pacific may also be noted. The importance of these streams has been more climatic than navigational and as such their absence has not materially affected the development of sea-going traffic in the Indian Ocean.

Partly perhaps as a result of the monsoons, and partly as a result of the earlier growth of civilisation, the Indian Ocean was undoubtedly the first centre of oceanic activity. The first naval and oceanic tradition in fact grew up in the lands washed by the Arabian sea. European writers, ignorant for the most part of even the main facts of Asiatic history, have assumed it as an axiom that navigational tradition first developed around the Aegean. Mackinder for example states "Modern research has made it plain that the leading sea-faring race of antiquity came at all times from that square of water between Europe and Asia which is known alternatively as the Aegean sea and the Archipelago, the chief sea of the Greeks. Sailors from this sea would appear to have taught the Phoenicians their trade . . .". Perhaps he was thinking in terms of the development of sea-faring traditions in Europe, but in terms of world history this statement is obviously inaccurate. Long before sea-faring developed in the limited Aegean waters, oceanic navigation had become common with the coastal people of Peninsula India.

Milleniums before Columbus sailed the Atlantic and Magellan crossed the Pacific, the Indian Ocean had become an active thoroughfare of commercial and cultural traffic. The close connection between the early civilisation of Nineveh and Babylon and the West Coast of India is borne out by indisputable evidence and this was possible only through the navigation of the Arabian sea. There is also ample evidence of a flourishing trade between the Levant and the West Coast of India, as may be inferred from allusions in the Old Testament. The analysis of the different products discovered in Mahenjo-daro (3,000-2,500 B.C.) has shown that many of them including gold came from the extreme south of India and could have only been transported by sea. Besides, much of the materials discovered in the remains of the Indus Valley civilisation came from the Red Sea coast, and other places outside India which fact also demonstrates that intimate commercial relations by way of the sea existed between India and the outside world even in those pre-historic times.

The earliest Indian literature, the Vedas (1,500 B.C.) speak of sea voyage. One well-known mantra (Rig Veda 1,97,8) prays : " Do thou convey us in a ship across the sea for our welfare." Besides this, there are numerous allusions in the Rig Veda to sea voyages and to ships with a hundred oars. In the Baberu Jataka (4th century B.C.) we are told of Indian merchants voyaging to Babylon. Prof. H. G. Rawlinson in his notable book on " Intercourse between India and the Western

World" has summarised the evidence available from European and other sources of the shipping activity in the Indian Ocean from the earliest times to the fall of Rome.

The voyages of the early navigators were no doubt along the coast. Dr. Perry and his school of anthropologists have shown that from the earliest times a sea-faring people had carried on activities along the entire coast line of the Indian Ocean. We have also definite evidence in the Obelisk of Shalmanesar III (860 B.C.) of the presence of Indian elephants in the valley of Euphrates. The Chaldeans navigated the coast in the eighth and ninth centuries before Christ and established a considerable naval power at Elam. The cities of the Elamites to the West of the Persian Gulf had under Merodach-baladan become a menace to Babylon by its sea power. *Sennachrib, we are told, had a fleet of great ships built "on the Phoenician model," for the purpose of fighting them. Sailing across the Gulf he invaded the Elamite coast and destroyed the power of the Chaldeans in their own harbours.

With Egypt, the relations of the West Coast were very intimate from the earliest times. The late Flinders Petrie discovered the portraits of Indian men and women at Memphis. He wrote: "These are the first remains of Indians on the Mediterranean we seem now to have touched the Indian Colony at Memphis."

Though the early navigators of the coast were of all races the Phoenicians, the Chaldeans and the Asiatic Greeks, the Hindus had the preponderant share, as earlier than all the rest they began sailing out into the open sea. Neither the Egyptians nor the Greeks sailed the Arabian Sea as they did not know the routes till Hippalus made the epoch-making discovery of the Monsoon winds in 45 A. D. But the Indian Navigators sailed across and had discovered Socotra (Sukhadhara) long before that time and navigated the Red Sea, as may be seen from the statement of Strabo that an Indian sailor who was found drifting in the Red Sea in a boat and was taken to Egypt offered to show the Egyptians the route to India.

* Seton Lloyd, *Twin Rivers*, p. 64.

This was in 120 B.C. 185 years before Hippalus' discovery. From Athaneus we know that there was very close connection between Egypt and India and that Ptolemy Philadelphus had in his procession many Indian women and that Indian spices were carried on camels.

The condition of navigation, the ports and the general geography of the Indian Ocean in the first century A.D. are described at length in Periplus Maris Erythraei. The names of dozens of Indian ports are mentioned most of which could be identified even now. But the most important statement from our point of view is that Red Sea ships on arrival at Broach (at the mouth of the Nerbadda) were met by the Government pilot boats and moored in regular basins.

With Hippalus' discovery of the monsoons, the navigation of the Indian Ocean underwent a revolutionary change. Egypt had become a Roman Province 75 years earlier (in 30 B.C.) and with the authority of the Empire established on the Isthmus, Roman trade with India had even before the time of Hippalus increased greatly in volume and range. We have Pliny's evidence that after the occupation of Egypt the Romans came "to control a compendious route whereby India was brought so near, that trade thither became very lucrative." The same author states that India, China and Arabia absorbed an enormous part of Roman currency. The discovery of great hordes of Roman coin in South India, especially on the West Coast, corroborates this statement.

Direct voyage from Aden to the Indian coast had not been tried by the Egyptians or Greeks and when Hippalus, following the wind, sailed direct to an Indian port he had, so far as the western nations were concerned, achieved a feat much more remarkable than what Vasco da Gama did 1,500 years later. The journey from Aden to the Malabar coast took only six weeks and consequently from that time onwards we have records of regular voyages between the Red Sea Ports and the Indian coast.

The numerous ports of India from Broach to Quilon became great markets of trade. A first century Tamil classic describes the port of Muziris (Cranganore in Cochin) as being filled with ships. The ruins of a Roman temple have also been discovered in that area. Such were the proportions of the Roman trade with the Malabar coast that in A.D. 408 Alaric was able to demand and receive 3,000 pounds of pepper which at that time and for nearly 1,400 years afterwards was practically the monopoly of Malabar.

The main races that used the sea at the time were undoubtedly the Hindus, Asiatic Greeks and the inhabitants of the Arabian coast line. The Hindus had already in use a magnetic compass known as *Matsya Yantra* for determining direction. The work " Merchants Treasure " written at Cairo by Baylak al Kiljaki mentions the magnetic needle as being in use in the Indian Ocean. Further, the Hindus had developed great skill in building ocean-going ships of great strength and durability. The participation of Hindus in the navigational activities of the Red Sea is also borne out by the *Oxyrhynchus Papyri, a second century farce in the Greek language in which the conversation between certain characters is in a language which has been identified by scholars as Canarese. Besides, there are extensive allusions to maritime affairs and to long voyages in early Tamil literature. Tamil scholars it is said, have counted no less than 1,800 nautical words in that language. It may, therefore, fairly be assumed that at the beginning of the Christian era the Arabian Sea was not only freely navigated by all the sea-going communities on the Indian coast line, but had become a regular highway of commercial and cultural traffic.

The evidence of deep sea navigation of the Bay of Bengal long before the Christian era is even more convincing. The undoubted existence of prosperous Hindu colonies in Malaya, Sumatra, Java and even Annam in the first century A.D. and the continuous communication with Indonesia which the mother country maintained clearly show that the Bay of Bengal had also been mastered long before that time. This was entirely an Indian achievement. Sylvain Lévi in " The Pre-

* Mukherji, *Indian Shipping*.

Ayran and Pre-Dravidian in India " states : *"The movement which carried Indian civilisation towards different parts of the globe about the beginning of the Christian Era was far from inaugurating any new route. Adventurers traffickers and missionaries profited by the technical progress of navigation " which had already become familiar. In the time of Asoka (third century B.C.) we have evidence of ships sailing from Tamralipti to Ceylon. One such vessel carried the historic mission of the Emperor's own sister, Sanghamitra for the conversion of the island. Buddhist Jatakas of the period preceding the Christian Era contain numerous stories of voyages to islands in the sea. For example, the Samudda Vanijja Jataka tells of a family which sailed down the Ganges into the sea at the winds' will until they reached an island that lay in the midst of the sea. Apart from coastal navigation it is now established that Kataha (Kedah) in the Malaya Peninsula was by this time a flourishing port of call for Indian sailors and a trading community, proving thereby that the crossing of the Bay between its widest points had been achieved long before that time.

* Page 125.

CHAPTER II

THE HINDU PERIOD IN THE INDIAN OCEAN

The control of the Indian seas belonged predominantly to India till the thirteenth century A.D. In respect of the Arabian Sea this was only a question of navigation. There was no colonising activity in that area, though Socotra, or Sukhadhara dwipa (the island of the blest) was discovered long before the Christian Era and was probably under Indian occupation at that time. Indian communities existed in Alexandria and other Egyptian towns and there were also settlements on the coasts of the Persian Gulf. But generally speaking, the navigation of the Arabian Sea was only for the purposes of trade.

It may be noted here, however, that the Northern Coast line of the Arabian Sea comes into Indian history for two notable instances of the influence of sea power on the shaping of events on land. Nearchus, the Greek Admiral transported the remnants of Alexander's weary hosts from the mouth of the Indus to the Persian Gulf in 323 B.C. It was a long and difficult trek over inhospitable regions that faced Alexander after the ruin of his hopes to conquer India, and the fate that overtook Napoleon and his Grand Army would undoubtedly have been shared by Alexanda, but for his decision to have ships built in India to transport his armies by the sea route. The other was the sea borne invasion of Sind which Bir Kassim carried out in the eight century A.D.

While however, it may be said that the Arabian Sea was used mainly for trade purposes, the case of the Bay of Bengal was different. The supremacy in that sea was naval and political, based on an extensive colonisation of the islands and it ceased only with the breakdown of Chola power in the thirteenth century as we shall now proceed to show.

The naval activity of the Hindus was controlled by organised corporations of which the most important were the Manigramam Chetties and the Nanadesis. Of the Manigramam Chetties who traded all over the world we have authentic records in grants and inscriptions. The Bhaskara Ravi Varman plate of the Kerala King grants certain special privileges to the Manigramam guild. *This body was given a charter practically similar to that given to the European East India Companies including "the sword of sovereign merchantship" and monopoly rights of trading. In an inscription discovered at Takopa near the Isthmus of Kra, the temple and tank of Sri Narayana are placed under the protection of this body of merchants. Other "merchant adventurers" known from records are the Nanadesis, the Valangai and the Elangai who are described in the inscription at Baligami in Mysore as bodies of †"brave men born to wander over many countries since the beginnings of the Krta age (the first in the Indian Cycle of Yugas) penetrating regions of the six continents by land and water routes, and dealing in various articles, such as horses and elephants, precious stones perfumes and drugs either wholesale or in retail."

It will be noticed that these corporations are described as being very ancient, dating fron time immemorial. Their activities are said to extend to six continents, and they use land and water routes for their commerce. It is recorded in another inscription that one of these corporations built a Vishnu Temple in Pegu which emphasises their predominantly Hindu character.

The idea that the Hindus had some kind of a ceremonial objection to the sea, while perhaps true in respect of the people of North India, was never true in respect of the people of the South. Peninsular India was maritime in its traditions and this is borne out also by Chinese records. Fa Hien writing in 415 A.D. states that in the ship which carried him from Ceylon to Sri Vijaya, there were two hundred merchants all of whom professed the brahminical religion.

* *Goda Varma: Bulletin of the School of Oriental Studies,* University of London, Vol. VIII, Part IV, 1937.

† *Epigraphica Carnatica,* Vol. VII; p. 118.

The ships used by these Hindu navigators at that time are described thus by Mr. J. Hornell stated to be an authority on Indian boat designs. They were *" square rigged, two masted vessels, with raked stem and stern, both sharp, without bowsprit and rudder and steered by two quarter paddles."

We have also texts which lay down detailed instructions about the construction of ocean-going vessels. The *Yukti Kalpa Taru* describes not only the construction of ships, but classifies them under different categories, such as those useful for inland navigation, for ocean voyages, for carrying goods and for carrying passengers. †Ten different kinds of ocean-going vessels are enumerated, the biggest of which, known as Vegini, is 176 cubits in length, 20 in breadth and 17$\frac{3}{8}$ in height. Cabined ships of different kinds meant for passenger traffic are also described as also those which were specially designed for naval warfare.

A description by Nicolo Conti in the earlier part of the fifteenth century shows that these instructions were not merely academic. He says: ‡" The natives of India build some ships larger than ours capable of containing 2,000 butts, and with five sails and as many masts. The lower part is constructed with triple planks in order to withstand the force of the tempests, to which they are much exposed. But some ships are so built in compartments that should one part be shattered the other portion remaining entire may accomplish the voyage."

Manu, the great law giver, provides in his Code, for shipping and port dues, while Kautalya's Arthasastra, an authoritative work on administration which was written in the fourth century B.C. lays down the functions of the Port Commissioner and Harbour Master. The Board of Shipping was one of the six great departments of the Mauryan Emperors. At the head of it was a Minister who dealt with all matters relating to shipping, including the navigation of the oceans. There was under him a staff of commissioners, harbour masters, etc.

* Quoted in *Towards Angkor* (Q. Wales), p. 26.

† Mukherji, *Indian Shipping*, p. 21-24.

‡ *India in the Fifteenth Century*, Kakliyt Society's Publications II, p. 27.

whose duty it was to look after ships in distress. As the Mauryan ports were mainly on the coast of the Bay of Bengal, this is conclusive evidence of the growth of trade and shipping in that sea as early as the fourth century B.C. In the first century A.D. also, both inscriptional and numismatical evidence shows that the Bay of Bengal was the centre of great maritime activity. *The Andhra Dynasty (which followed the Mauryas) whose territories also bordered on the Bay of Bengal has left some remarkable coins with pictures of ships on them. As this was the great period of the first colonisation of Java, Sumatra and other islands in the Pacific, these coins were most probably struck to proclaim the supremacy of the seas which the Andhra Emperors then enjoyed, as even Dr. Vincent Smith recognises.

We have also evidence of regular maritime traffic by the Hindus in the South China seas before the Christian era. At the beginning of that period both Chinese records and the Greek Geographer Ptolemy record the existence of Indian colonies in the present territory of Indo-China. An inscription in Takopa in the southern tip of Siam shows that a Hindu Trading community known as *Manigramam* which had its centres also in Malabar, as we know from copper-plate grants of Bhaskar Ravi Varman already alluded to, acted as trustees for a temple of Naravana. The growth of large Hindu Kingdoms and Empires in Champa (Siam) Cambodia, Java, Sumatra and other areas in Indonesia and their full-fledged and constantly renovated Hindu and Buddhist culture for a period of at least seven hundred years from the fifth to the thirteenth centuries, demonstrate beyond doubt the close relations between the mother country and the colonies based on uninterrupted sea traffic. The sea ports on the East coast maintained regular shipping services as is established not only from the frequent references to such travel in the Katha Sarit Sagara and other works but in records of the Chinese Travellers.

From at least the fifth century B.C. to the sixth century A.D. this naval supremacy rested with the continental powers in

* Rae, *South Indian Buddhist Antiquities* : *Archaeological Survey of India.* N.I.S. XV.

India. First the Marrvas and then the Andhras were the lords of the Eastern Seas. Kalidasa alludes to the Kings of Bengal having sea-going fleets and the Andhra ports being filled with ships carrying spices from the East. From the Andhras the sovereignty of the Eastern Seas passed to the Pallavas as may be inferred from the great influence which this dynasty exercised on the colonial kingdoms of Further India. The inscriptions of Cambodia and Java are in Pallava characters; the architecture of the period is distinctly inspired by Pallava achievements and in fact Pallava leadership is writ large in the history of Java, Champa (Siam) and Cambodia in the seventh, eighth and ninth centuries.

Though the first voyages might have been along the coast-line of the Bay, we have definite and conclusive proof of oceanic voyages of South Indian ships. The route that Fa Hien, the celebrated Chinese monk, took to return home after his stay in India (412-413) is fully described by him. Leaving Tram-ralipti, the Orissa port, he took fourteen days to reach Ceylon. From there he embarked for Java and called at Nicobars (Nak- kavaram), the island of the naked. From Nicobars the ship passed through the Straits of Malacca into the Pacific. Oceanic travel was therefore well advanced in the fifth century and Indian mariners not merely crossed the Bay of Bengal at its widest point, but sailed far out into the Pacific.

We have also historical evidence of some of the continental powers using their naval power for purposes of conquest. Pulikesin II the Chalukya King who reigned in the first half of the seventh century led a naval expedition, which rounding Cape Comorin sailed up to the coast of Orissa and reduced the city of Puri, the capital of the Kalinga Kings who had for long been the chief naval power in the Bay of Bengal. The Pandyas, Cholas and others also maintained powerful navies, while the Rulers of Malabar exercised naval sway over the seas of the Western coast.

From the fifth century to the tenth the command of the Malacca Straits was in the hands of a great Indian naval power, based on Sumatra known to history as the Sri Vijaya

Empire. This State included much of Peninsular Malaya, Sumatra and the Western half of Java besided numerous island principalities. I'Tsing who resided for some years in that Kingdom says that the King possessed numerous ships which sailed regularly between India and Sri Vijaya as also between Sumatra and China.

The Sri Vijaya Kings maintained a powerful navy which swept the sea of pirates and corsairs. Their naval power, well attested by their continuous raids on the coasts of Champa and Annam are recorded both in local inscriptions and Chinese annals. (e.g. Po Nagar Stelae inscription of King Satya Varman 784 A.D. and in Yang Tikuh inscription of Indra Varman I, dated 787). With the Straits of Malacca firmly under their control and with their authority extending over the far flung group of islands, the Sri Vijaya Kings were in a position to enforce their rule of the Indian waves. Further, they were also closely connected with the Indian Kingdoms on the Western side of the Bay especially with the Kalinga monarchs of Orissa. Inscriptions on the mainland, e.g. the Nalanda copper plate of the time of Devapala, show that frequent intercourse was maintained by this Empire with the Kingdoms of India.

Till the end of the tenth century, that is, for a period of nearly 500 years, the Sri Vijaya Kings were the Lords of the Ocean. But in 1007 the Chola Emperor Rajendra fitted out a powerful navy and challenged the might of Sri Vijaya. He not only defeated the opposing navy, but captured Kedah and established the Chola power on the Malaya Peninsula. Numerous inscriptions bear witness to this fact. Having created a base on the Eastern side of the sea and extended their rule over the Peninsula, the Cholas carried on war against the Sri Vijaya Kings in their own home waters. This naval rivalry lasted for nearly 100 years. Though the Sri Vijaya Kings were forced for long to fight on the defensive, their power, based on the islands and controlling the Straits, could not be destroyed even by the overwhelming might of the Cholas. It is the Chola power that found the burden too heavy to carry especially as it was being continuously subjected to attack by its neighbours in India. From their profitless overseas adventure the Cholas finally withdrew by the end of the century.

This hundred years naval war was of great importance. It weakened the Sri Vijaya power and opened the way for the Moslem supremacy in Indian waters. But the downfall of Hindu naval power did not come till the destruction of the Sri Vijaya Empire in the fourteenth century. Chau Ju Kua, the Imperial Chinese Inspector of Foreign Trade, in his work entitled *Chu Fau Chi written in 1225 states that Sri Vijaya was not merely a great emporium of trade, but controlled the Straits of Malacca and thus was able to dominate the sea trade of China with the west. All ships passing through the Straits had to call at the capital and the maritime administration kept watch on traffic through the lane.

That the naval power of Sri Vijaya continued till the middle of the thirteenth century is clearly established by two invasions of Ceylon which Chandrabhanu the King of Sri Vijaya undertook in 1236 and 1256 respectively. The Ceylon record Culla Vamsa, a continuation of the famous annals, Maha Vamsa, states as follows:

In the 11th year of King Parakrama Bahu II a king of Chavaka named Chandrabhanu landed with an army at Kakkala. His soldiers treacherously occupied the passages across the rivers and having defeated all who opposed them devastated the whole of Ceylon. But the Regent Virabahu defeated them in several battles and forced them to withdraw. A few years later King Chandrabhanu again landed at Mahathirtha and his army was on this occasion reinforced by a large number of Pandya Chola and other Tamil soldiers. The second enterprise though it was supported by allies from the mainland did not meet with success. After gaining some initial success the allies were defeated and driven out of Ceylon.

* *Records of Foreign Nations*, translated by Heith and Rockhill, St. Petersburg, 1911.

The unfortunate Chandrabhanu met with a tragic end. He was attacked by his erstwhile ally the Pandya Ruler, who records in his inscription of 1264 that he conquered and killed the King of Chavaka.

The great expeditions of Chandrabhanu involving a combined action of many thousand soldiers and hundreds of ships across the Bay of Bengal constitute the last chapter in Hindu oceanic supremacy. After his defeat and death in the battle with Vira Pandya the Sri Vijaya Kingdom ceases to be a naval power, though it continued as an island State for another hundred years.

Though their power was based on Sumatra and Malaya the Sri Vijaya Kings were new South Indian colonists. Apart from the close political relations which existed between them and the South Indian maritime Kingdoms of Chola, Pandya and Kerala, we have inscriptions in Sri Vihaya which describe the activities of South Indian commercial corporations like the Fifteen Hundred and Manigramam. In many of the inscriptions the South Indian Grantha character is used. Further, many of the clan names in Sumatra are the same as in the South of India, i.e. Cholas, Pandyas, Malaya, etc.

The period of Hindu supremacy in the Ocean was one of complete freedom of trade and navigation. While pirates were extirpated and the routes kept open, there was no interference of any kind with trade which was open to ships of all nations. For example, we have the statement of Abdur Razzak (1442) that at Calicut every ship whatever place it might have come from or wherever it might be bound for, when it put into this port was treated like other vessels and had no trouble of any kind to put up with. The Arabs freely navigated the seas, traded with Indian ports and even carried their cargoes as far East as China, as their own records prove. Periplus noticed them in the first century A.D. The Chinese junks made their appearance in the Indian seas in the fourth century. There was evidently no question of monopoly or exclusion of others from free traffic on the seas.

After the downfall of Sri Vijaya and the disappearance of

the Cholas from the stage of Indian history, Oceanic trade in the Indian seas passed almost exclusively to Arab hands. It is true that the powerful kings of the West Coast, especially the Rulers of Gujerat and Calicut maintained considerable navies and their ships sailed with cargoes to the West, the Persian Gulf, Arabia and the East Coast of Africa. But the supremacy of the oceanic routes had passed defiinitely to the Arabs. They were the great carriers of Indian trade in the fourteenth and fifteenth centuries and their activities extended from the Red Sea ports to Canton and the marts of China. With the Indian potentates on the coast and with the Indian traders in the ports they maintained the happiest relations. There was no attempt at any time of exercising a naval control, perhaps as a result of the fact that Arab navigation was not the outcome of any State policy, but was developed through centuries thanks to activities of merchant adventurers, as in the case of the Hindus in the period immediately preceding.

The Arabs were the great intermediaries of trade between Europe and India. From the marts on the Red Sea Coast the Venetians who had the control of the Mediterranean carried the goods to markets of the west. The Genoese and the Iberian nations were intensely jealous of the prosperity of Venice and of her monopoly of the Indian trade. They were actively exploring a direct passage to India, and this was the motive animating the great maritime activity of the second half of the fifteenth century which led to the rounding of the Cape, the discovery of America and the voyage of Vasco da Gama to India.

CHAPTER III

THE ARRIVAL OF THE EUROPEANS

It may seem strange, but it is none the less true, that till the last decade of the fifteenth century none of the European nations, except perhaps the Vikings had ventured into oceanic navigation. The navigational activities of the European peoples were confined to inland seas like the Mediterranean, the North Sea and the Baltic and to the coasts of Europe. Only the Hindus, the Chinese and the Arabs had developed a tradition of oceanic navigation and of these, as we noticed before, the Hindus had the largest share till the end of the thirteenth century.

The dominant motive which led to the great maritime adventures of the end of the fifteenth century was the desire to establish a direct route to India and thereby to outflank the land power which controlled the Isthmus. Henry the Navigator, the inspirer of the great discoveries and the pioneer of oceanic navigation in Europe occupied Ceuta in 1415. His second expedition against Tangier in 1437 ended in disaster, the Infant Dom Fernand himself being made prisoner by the Berbers. Prince Henry dreamed of a direct route to India and received from Pope Nocolas V and Calixtus III bulls giving to the Portuguese the rights of their future discovery.

It is significant that the islands of Madeira lying so near to the Portuguese coast were only discovered in the fifteenth century and Prince Henry's own navigations were also confined to the coasts of Africa. But he sailed down that coast farther than others and thereby opened the way for Barthelmy Diaz who in 1487 discovered the Cape of the Tempests, which as it was hoped would open the route to India was renamed the Cape of Good Hope. Compared to what the Indian and Arab navigators had achieved in sailing across uncharted seas, Diaz's voyage down the coast of Africa, following the line of the shore was in no way remarkable, but compared to the records of European navigation up to the time it was no doubt unique. In any case it was epoch-making, as a direct route to India was thereby rendered possible.

The expedition for continuing the work of Diaz and reaching India was entrusted to Vasco da Gama, who sailed from Belem near Lisbon on the 8th of July, 1497 on the *San Gabriel*, a vessel of less than 120 tons. It was only in December that da Gama arrived in Moussel Bay at the southern end of Africa. In March 1498 he put in at Mozambique, then an important Arab trading centre of the African coast. There he re-victualled his ships and obtained the services of a pilot who helped in the navigation up to Melinde, the regular port of departure for the coast of India. At Melinde Vasco da Gama was able to obtain the services of a Malabar Hindu, with full knowledge of the winds and the route. The season was also favourable. The first monsoon winds had begun to blow and the *San Gabriel* steered by the Malabar Hindu reached Calicut on the 11th May 1498, crossing the Arabian sea in a voyage of twenty days.

The *San Gabriel* and her two consorts were indeed small ships. But significantly enough they carried heavy arms. The flag ship carried 20 guns, a mighty portent for the future of the sea, which was free till then. The two consorts were also equally well armed and apart from the crew the men who accompanied da Gama were trained soldiers.

Of the voyage as a feat of navigation, I have elsewhere written as follows:—

> "The discovery of the sea-route to India was a great event from the point of view of the results that followed from it. But as a feat of exploration, or even of nautical adventure, it was of no importance.
>
> "The historical results that have flowed from the direct contact of European Powers with India and the commerce and wealth which the control of the Indian seas has given to Europe, have shed an exaggerated light on Vasco's achievement. It should be remembered that the project

of a voyage to India round the Cape did in no sense originate with Vasco da Gama. He had in fact nothing to do with the conception or the planning of the project. It had already been planned by Dom Joao following the traditional policy of Dom Henry; and in this Dom Joao had at his disposal the expert advice of Abraham Ben Zakut. Even the instructions to Gama were drawn up in consultation with him. The discovery of the Cape of Good Hope by Diaz had partially fulfilled the dream of Dom Joao; and the plan itself was matured and its organisation undertaken by Dom Manuel, on the basis of authentic information gathered by the court during half a century of exploration. Moreover, India was in no sense a *terra incognita*. It was in close contact with Europe, through the Venetians and the Moors. Besides, the seafaring people on the Coast of Africa, consisting mainly of Arabian settlers, knew the routes and the winds, and da Gama had the help of competent Arab pilots supplied to him by the King of Melinde. He was not sailing in charted seas like Columbus or Magellan, but sailing along recognised routes to a country which was situated at a known distance from the African coast. There is nothing in Vasco da Gama's discovery which entitles him to the claim of a great explorer or navigator. His glory is based entirely on the historical results that followed, for which he was hardly responsible."

The significance of da Gama's entry into the Indian Sea lies not in the navigational achievement, but in the policy of the Portuguese kings who looked upon the seas as their possession. The twenty guns that the *San Gabriel* carried announced the claim of the Portuguese king based on the Papal Bull giving him exclusive dominion in Asia and Africa.

The first voyage was merely exploratory. Gama had expressed to the Zamorin, as the King of Calicut is styled, only a desire to trade with him, but his refusal to pay the customs of the port was an indication of the policy he had in mind. The second expedition under Cabral was on a much larger scale. It consisted originally of 33 ships and carried 1,500 men but only 6 vessels reached India.

Cabral had definite views as to the rights of the Portuguese on the sea. As Barroes states: *" It is true that there does exist a common right to all to navigate the seas and in Europe we recognise the rights which others hold against us; *but this right does not extend beyond Europe and therefore the Portuguese as Lords of the Sea are justified in confiscating the goods of all those who navigate the seas without their permission.*"

This was an unequivocal and uncompromising claim to the complete monopoly of the seas *in peace time* and Cabral proceeded to enforce it. But the determined opposition of the Zamorin whose sea power was considerable led to Cabral's abandonment of that port after a brutal bombardment of the city, and to his settlement later at Cochin.

The challenge to the Zamorin's naval power was not left unanswered. The Ruler of Calicut fitted out a fleet 80 ships strong carrying 1,500 men. The " Lord of the Sea " considered discretion to be the better part of valour and hastily sailed away on sighting the Calicut ships.

Though Cabral had sailed away, the Portuguese had not abandoned the Indian Ocean. They came to have a greater realisation of the difficulties facing them and the inglorious retreat of Cabral only convinced Dam Manuel of the necessity of further effort and greater preparations. The Portuguese King therefore sent out a stronger expedition with orders to enforce his claim as the Lord of the Indian sea. Dom Manuel assumed for himself the title of " the Lord of the navigation conquest and commerce of Ethiopia, Arabia, Persia and India." It was da Gama himself who led that third expedition which was to proclaim to the people of Asia the sovereignty of the Portuguese over the Indian Ocean.

The Armada of which da Gama was appointed Captain Major consisted of 15 ships of which six, including *San Jeronymo*, the flag ship, were larger than any that had so far sailed the Indian seas. The other five were lateen rigged

* Barroes, Vol. 1, Book I.

caravels fitted with heavy artillery and the expedition carried 800 trained soldiers. Realising that there might be serious opposition, a reinforcement of 5 vessels under Estavo da Gama was sent a month and a half later.

Of the numerous acts of piracy committed by da Gama and his associates during this voyage it is unnecessary to speak. Only one incident quoted in *Lendas da India*, typical of many, will show the state of civilisation of these Lords of Navigation. Capturing some unarmed ships returning from Mecca the Captain Major "after making the ships empty of goods prohibited any one from taking out of it any Moor and then ordered them to set fire to it." In the history of piracy it will be difficult to find a parallel to the barbarism of this Portuguese hero.

The Zamorin was prepared to meet this challenge. His fleet under Kassim decided to attack the Portuguese Armada anchored off Cochin. Apart from his own fast small vessels Kassim was reinforced by a fleet of heavier vessels belonging to Khoja Ambar, a Red Sea trader of great wealth and influence. Though the Calicut fleet had the advantage of speed, fire power was on the side of the Portuguese. In the engagement that followed Khoja Ambers heavier ships suffered greatly as a result of Portuguese fire, but Vasco da Gama found that the small fast vessels of Calicut were more than a match for his own armed caravels, and after an indecisive engagement, escaped with his ships to Europe.

Though the honours of the battle off Cochin (1503) lay with the Calicut navy, the failure of Kassim to destroy the Portuguese fleet and his inability to chase da Gama nullified the fruits of his victory. In fact the Calicut navy was in no way a high sea fleet as it consisted mainly of fast small vessels. Near the coast they could meet the Portuguese on more than equal terms, but they were unsuited for operations at any distance from their base. The failure of Kassim to force a decision when he had the superiority was disastrous, as it showed to the Portuguese the essential weakness of the

Zamorin's sea power. In that sense it was one of the more important engagements in Indian history.

Hardly had da Gama left the Indian Ocean, when another fleet of 14 ships under Lopo Soares arrived in Indian waters. Soares was an experienced captain and in a surprise attack he destroyed a squadron of the Calicut force which under Mammali was lying at anchor off Cranganore. Then he proceeded to attack a mercantile fleet which had assembled in another port and dispersed it after a hard-fought struggle with its protecting convoy. The Zamorin now realised that against the heavily armed Portuguese caravels, his own ships stood but little chance in ranged action. He invoked the aid of the Sultan of Egypt with whom he was in friendly relations. An Egyptian fleet carrying no less than 1500 men and equipped with the latest weapons sailed into the Arabian sea under an experienced Admiral, Mir Hussain, early in 1507. Mir Hussain's strategy was simple and sound. His first objective was the island of Diu which he decided to use as his base, and effecting a junction with the navy of the Zamorin the combined fleet was to attack the Portuguese.

The Portuguese Viceroy at the time, Don Francesco d'Almeida, was a man of remarkable foresight and ability whose genius had been overshadowed by his rival and successor Albuquerque. A great nobleman with influence at Court he was definitely opposed to any policy of conquest, but he had a full appreciation of the importance of unchallenged mastery of the Indian seas for the future of the Portuguese in Asia. Though an officer of the land forces, with a brilliant record of warfare in Morocco, he wanted the absolute control of the sea and knew well that all his schemes for a Commercial Empire in the East depended on achieving that control.

Hussain reached Diu immediately after the monsoon. The Zamorin's vessels joined him there and the combined forces moved south. The Portuguese navy under Loureneco d' Almeida, the son of the Viceroy, sailed north from their base in Cochin to meet this new threat. The two fleets met at Chaul, halfway down the coast. It was mainly a war of artillery as the Portuguese attempts to board the Egyptian vessels failed. After two days of cannonading the Portuguese decided to flee, but the flag ship of d' Almeida was hit and the captain himself was killed.

Disaster faced the Portuguese. An enemy who was equal in equipment and superior in seamanship had arrived on the Indian waters and at that moment the dream of Dom Manuel had almost become a nightmare. But the Viceroy, Don Francesco d' Almeida did not lose heart. Collecting every available ship and all the arms he could lay hands on, Don Francesco sailed north to meet the enemy. He had with him 18 ships and 1200 men. Reaching Diu on the 2nd of February 1509, Almeida awaited the Indo-Egyptian forces Here treachery favoured him. Malik Aiyaz, a European convert who was the King of Gujerat's Governor in Diu, secretly joined the Portuguese and deprived Mir Hussain of his supplies. The Egyptian Admiral had to fall back for his supplies on the 100 vessels that the Zamorin had sent. Besides his own effective fleet, apart from the Calicut auxiliaries, consisted only of 10 ships. In spite of these disadvantages Mir Hussain decided to give battle. On February the 3rd, 1509, the opposing fleets met off Diu. Again as an engagement it was inconclusive. Neither side could claim victory, but disgusted with the treachery of the Sultan of Gujerat the Egyptian fleet sailed away shortly afterwards.

Thus without a decisive battle, the supremacy of the sea passed to the Portuguese. Judged from results the battle off Cochin in 1503, and the engagement off Diu in 1509 are the two most significant events in Indian history. The first action showed to the Portuguese the weakness of the Indian navies and afforded them the opportunity for building up a naval Empire. The second left them free to pursue any oceanic policy they desired and laid the firm foundation of the European mastery of the Eastern seas which has now continued for over 400 years. In that sense they are fundamentally more important than Plassey or Buxar for the future history of India.

CHAPTER IV

PORTUGUESE SEA POWER

With the departure of Mir Hussain and the Egyptian fleet from the Indian waters in 1509 the Portuguese may be said to have established supremacy in the Indian Ocean. It should not however be understood that so far as the coasts of India were concerned, the " Lords of Navigation " had undisputed mastery. For well over 90 years the Zamorin's fleet held its own in the home waters of Calicut. For a description of this epic struggle between the Admirals of Calicut and the Portugese Captains reference may be made to " Malabar and the Portuguese." Under a succession of able and intrepid commanders the Malabar fleet kept up an unceasing struggle keeping the Portuguese away from the Calicut coast and harassing them at every turn.

The naval history of this period especially in its relation to the Portuguese claim to exclusive navigation is dominated by a remarkable family of Malabar Muslims who were for a century the hereditary admirals of the Zamorin's fleet. The Zamorin's title was the Lord of the Mountains and the Waves. For over 500 years the Rulers of Calicut had maintained without challenge that claim to the sovereignty of the Malabar sea. The Red Sea trade which followed the Monsoon was especially under their protection. With the ports on the Persian Gulf and on the African coast they maintained close contact. The Sultans of Gujerat and the Rulers of the Konkan coast recognised the primacy of the Zamorin in the southern waters.

The family of Calicut Admirals is known to history as Ali Marrakkars. Their headquarters and naval station were situated at Ponnani, a naturally strong harbour to the south of Calicut. Later when the fight with the Portuguese developed the Marakkars moved to Kottakkal where they built a strong base protected by a fortress with dockyards and other facilities.

During the hundred years of war with the Portuguese this family produced a succession of four remarkable sea captains, whose prowess makes the name of " Malabar Pirates " resound still in history. In initiative, courage, navigational skill and persistence they bear comparison with the great figures of naval warfare. Undoubtedly in the manner of the period they were ruthless, cared but little for the rights of others, but compared to their Portuguese opponents, they were humane and civilised. They were never responsible for the kind of atrocities that Gama and his successors committed. Especially it may be said of Kunjali III that in spite of a lifetime of the most determined warfare in which both sides neither received nor gave quarter, he was a model of chivalry, considerate in ordinary life, a cultivated nobleman, a knight in the language of the Portuguese.

The following events may be noted. Ponnani, the southern naval station of the Zamorin was stormed by the Portuguese in 1524. In the same year Kuttiali the Calicut admiral attacked Lope Vaz de Sampayo off Cannanore and drove him away from the Malabar seas. In 1528 a determined effort was made to destroy the Zamorin's fleet and though Kuttiali was captured, his son and successor Kunjali II carried on the struggle with even greater vigour. Kunjali carried the war into enemy territory and did not hesitate to attack Portuguese possessions in Ceylon. The Calicut fleet established itself at Kote and supporting the rights of one of the claimants in the civil war continuously attacked the Portuguese for a period of over seven years. Kunajli is reported by Portuguese historians as having captured no less that 50 ships in one year and the Lords of the Sea were hard put to maintain their coastal lines of communication.

The Zamorin however, realised that it was a losing game and that the only chance of freeing the sea from the authority of Portugal was to secure the help of an equally great naval power. He entered into negotiations with Turkey and an alliance was signed between the Kings of Cambay and Calicut and the Sultan of Turkey. In pursuance of this arrangement

Suleiman Pasha Al Khadim the Governor of Egypt received the following instructions from Sultan Suleiman the Magnificent:

> "You who are the begler beg of Egypt, Suleiman Pasha immediately on receipt of my orders will get ready your bag and baggage and make preparations in Suez for a holy war and having equipped and supplied a fleet and collected a sufficient army you will set out for India and capture and hold those ports cutting off the road and blocking the way to Mecca and Medina, you will avert the evil deeds of the Portuguese infidels and remove their flag from the sea."

It was in 1538 that Suleiman arrived in India. Kunjali in the meantime was carrying on a running fight with the Portuguese. In 1537 he rounded the Cape Comorin and attacked the settlement at Negapatam where the unexpected appearance of a squadron upset his plans. Nothing daunted he appeared again on the sea with a new fleet which Martim de Souza the Governor had the greatest difficulty in bringing to action, as it was Kunjali's policy to avoid decisive engagements. But on the 20th Febraury, 1538, when the Turkish fleet was approaching India, de Souza was able to force Kunjali to fight an action which, though it failed to destroy the Zamorin's sea power, helped him to get the sea cleared for a short time. Martim de Souza was free to sail north to meet the Turk. Suleiman Pasha, however, did not fight, but returned in haste to Egypt.

After the return of Suleiman Pasha there was a short truce in the naval war. But the Portuguese failed to keep the terms and the Zamorin again took up the attack. The settlement at Panicale on the East coast was attacked, taken and sacked by Kunjali, who following the traditional policy of the Calicut Rulers avoided battle unless forced to, but preyed on Portuguese shipping and trade. No naval action of any consequence took place till 1558, Kunjali eluding the Portuguese for no less than 15 years, while keeping the Calicut coast clear of enemy ships. In 1558, Luiz de Mello was able to force an action off

Cannanore. Kunjali's fleet consisted of 13 vessels and the action was a hard fought engagement. The flag ship of Kunjali was sunk and three others were captured, but the other nine retired unmolested to Calicut.

Luiz de Mello decided after this to destroy the Zamorin's fleet by a blockade of the Calicut coast. With a powerful fleet of 30 ships carrying over 600 men he appeared off Calicut. The traditional strategy of the Portuguese commanders since the time of da Gama was to chase the Malabar fleet and force it to fight a decisive action. This time de Mello decided on a change. He split up his forces and blocked the river mouths, while the commander himself sailed up and down enforcing the blockade. If this policy had been pursued for any length of time, the Calicut fleet would have been completely destroyed, but de Mello was recalled and the blockade was lifted.

This gave Kunjali another chance. One of his captains appeared suddenly on the East coast, with some galleons and forty sloops (1553). The Portuguese had a settlement at Punney Kayal and the Calicut commander boldly effected a landing which was hotly contested by the garrison. Manuel Rodrigo de Continho who was the captain of the factory retired with his men and took shelter inside the fort which the Calicut commander attacked and captured. A force had to be sent from Cochin to drive off the Zamorin's forces.

The war flared up again in 1564. The Calicut forces destroyed the Portuguese ships in the harbour of Cannanore and this awoke the Viceroy in Goa from his torpor. A large fleet under Goncalo Marmanaque was ordered down the Malabar coast with instructions to destroy the power of the Zamorin. Marmanaque divided his fleet into three squadrons, the major portion under himself blockading the Malabar coast, while a squadron under Dom Paulo de Lenia was stationed in the Bay of Bhatkal. A third squadron under Pedro de Silva with seven ships had the duty of general patrol. Following up his success the Malabar admiral evaded Marmanaque and attacked Dom Paulo in the Bay of Bhatkal and gained a complete victory, Dom Paulo himself being wounded in the action.

Kunjali's aggressive activities following this victory became so great a menace that the Viceroy Conde de Atouquiera despatched in 1569 a large fleet of 36 vessels under an experienced captain, Dom Martino de Miranda. Kunjali again tried to evade a decisive action and kept up his harassing tactics and the Portuguese captain was so exasperated by these methods that he accepted a fight in an unfavourable position. The result was a notable victory for Kunjali. De Miranda was wounded and had to be carried off to Cochin where he died.

After this the Malabar fleet was in a position to take the offensive. Kunjali sailed up as far north as Diu where he gained another victory over a squadron commanded by Ruy Dias Cabral and Henrique de Menses, the former being killed and the latter taken prisoner.

The naval war continued uninterrupted, the Malabar navy holding its own and keeping the enemy away from the Calicut coast at least so long as Kunjali III lived. The great Admiral passed away in 1595. The hero of a thousand fights who defied the naval might of Portugal for over 40 years and whose knightly courtliness is attested to even by his enemies. Kunjali III was undoubtedly one of the greatest figures in Indian Naval history, a figure of romance, valour and adventure.

Kunjali was not only an old sea dog, the hero of a hundred fights, but also a great organiser, The ease with which he put successive fleets on the sea and kept up the fight continuously in spite of the most determined efforts of the Portuguese for a period of 40 years bears witness to his resourcefulness and skill. No sooner was one fleet destroyed, captured or dispersed and the Portuguese Viceroys heaved a sigh of relief than a new and more powerful fleet arrived on the waters to carry on the fight. After the experince of Khoja Ambar, the Malabar Admirals had learnt the lesson that against the heavily armed Portuguese it was useless to put heavy ships of unequal armament. The Malabar vessels were all of the Parao type built lightly for speed, fast sailing and easily manageable. Any number of them could be constructed without difficulty, for timber was in plenty and ship-building was a hereditary craft for which Malabar artisans were famous.

Kunjali's methods on the sea were simple. The speed of his vessels enabled him to appear at the most unexpected places. One day he would be seen off the isolated Portuguese settlements on the East coast, harassing merchantmen, capturing stragglers and attacking outposts. By night he would sail away after other quarry, sailing patiently behind powerful convoys, for a suitable opportunity for attack. His speed enabled him to refuse action except when weather and position favoured him.

When forced to fight his tactics were to surround single vessels by forcing his crafts among the lined Portuguese ships. Of all the seamen known to naval history, Kunjali III was most akin to Andrea Doria the Venetian Commander who was forced by circumstances to carry on an unequal fight against the Turkish navy. Their position was similar. The Turkish navy in the middle of the sixteenth century was overwhelmingly powerful in the Mediterranean. It was impossible for Doria to challenge the might of Khaireddin. His resources were much less that those of his opponent. His ships were less heavily equipped and the bases and stations open to him were limited. But Doria fought a ceaseless struggle against the great Khaireddin practically by the same tactics as Kunjali used.

The restricted activities of the Malabar fleet in no way affected the oceanic supremacy of Portugal. The only time when it was seriously challenged was when Mir Hussain's Egyptian fleet occupied Diu and destroyed Lorenco d' Almeida's squadron in the battle of Chaul. But Hussain's withdrawal in 1509 left the supremacy of the high seas to the Portuguese. Within seven months of Mir Hussain's departure Affonso Albuquerque had assumed office as Governor. It was the genius and foresight of this one man which laid the foundation of Europe's Empire in Asia.

Albuquerque is one of the few landsmen in history who have shown an equal talent in oceanic and naval affairs.

Among others in a lesser degree may be mentioned Prince Rupert and Blake. But he was much more than an admiral with an appreciation of oceanic policies. A statesman and administrator of the highest order he could legitimately claim to have been a great Empire builder, one who has consciusly changed the course of history, and determined on a large scale the shape of events to come.

Born of an aristocratic family in Lisbon in 1462, Albuquerque claimed to have royal blood in his veins, though it was counted through at least two illegitimacies on the maternal side. From his childhood he was brought up in the immediate circle of the court, as the playmate and companion of Prince John. Like others of noble blood he joined the army early in his youth and took part in the campaigns in Africa against the Moors. During the last quarter of the fifteenth century the African campaigns of Portugal provided undoubtedly the best school of training for officers and statesmen. It is noteworthy that almost all the great figures of Portuguese history in its great period, including the poet Luiz Camoens had seen service in Africa against the Moors. In his short military career Albuquerque not merely showed courage and qualities of leadership, but achieved distinction by capturing the fortress of Arzila.

When Dom John became King, Affonso was appointed Master of the House and later on a member of the Kings Personal Guard. Albuquerque, however, was not a favourite with Manuel the Fortunate who suceeded John and he was sent out to India where another career awaited him.

Unlike his predecessors Albuquerque was familiar with the Indian Ocean and had a knowledge of its problems before he took up his post. In 1506 he accompanied Tristan da Cunha on an expedition in which he piloted his own ship. The object of the expedition was to stop the vessels entering and leaving the Red Sea, but he also carried with him a secret patent of appointment as Governor on the retirement of Almeida which was to take place three years later. This first service in the Gulf of Aden, one of the most important strategic areas in the Indian Ocean, was of very great significance. Albuquerque recognising the importance of Socotra for the control of the main route fron the Red Sea and the Arabian coast seized it without hesitation, built a fort there and converted it into a great naval base. He stayed on in those waters even after da Cunha left, and his next object was Ormuz which controlled the Persian Gulf and thereby commanded the trade route between India and Persia. Acting on his own and without any authority from any one, Albuquerque demanded and obtained the tribute of the King of Ormuz after a short bombardment of the city. He entered into a treaty with the Ruler of Ormuz which is the prototype and forerunner of the treaty system with country powers which the British took over with such effect, in the eighteenth and ninteenth centuries. The King of Ormuz was to retain his independence under the protection of the Portuguese fort, and he was prohibited from entering into relations with any hostile power. The European Empire in Asia was thus born on October the 24th 1506 when the Fort of Ormuz was built and the King declared a tributary of Portugal.

When shortly after Mir Hussain sailed away Albuquerque became the Governor, the Portuguese had at the head of the affairs in India one who had an oceanic mind, which had already decided on the plans for a complete and undisturbed mastery of the Indian seas. His first idea was to create an impregnable base in Malabar by the reduction of the Zamorin whose sea power so near the Portuguese headquarters at Cochin seemed to him a perpetual menace. He, therefore, decided to attack Calicut, but in this effort he was foiled. Albuquerque himself was not in favour of a direct attack, but Marshal Couthino who had arrived in India had rashly promised the King of Portugal to bring the person of the Zamorin in triumph to Lisbon. An expedition was fitted out and Albuquerque landed at Calicut with a strong force commanded by a Marshal of Portugal, Dom Fernando Coutinho in January 1510. The reduction of Calicut was however, no easy matter. The Portuguese expeditionary force was cut to pieces, the Marshal himself with 70 fidalgos fell on the field, and the Portuguese banner became a trophy of the Zamorin. Albuquerque himself received two wounds, one on the left arm and another on the neck. A cannon shot felled him to the ground and he was carried unconscious to his ship. The first move in his great plan thus ended in disaster.

The defeat at Calicut had far-reaching results. Albuquerque was now convinced that Cochin was too near the power of the Zamorin to form a safe base for his imperial plans. Looking around he selected Goa, as it had an excellent harbour, a suitable hinterland which could be easily held and, what was more, was sufficiently far away from any Ruler with a strong enough navy. It was in fact halfway between Gujerat and Calicut. Goa was easily taken at the first assault on 27th February 1510, but here also Albuquerque had underestimated the power of the Indian Rulers. He was driven out by a counter attack. Returning six months later, he captured it after a fight, and took a terrible vengence on the population. As he himself boasts in his letter to the King: "afterwards, I burnt the city and put all to the sword . . . . whenever we could find them no Moor was spared, and they filled the mosques with them and set them on fire."

Goa provided an ideal base for Albuquerque's schemes. "The Governor has now turned the key of India in his King's favour," Castenhada quotes a Cochin merchant as stating. A great fort was built there and arrangements made for permanent government. Albuquerque could now legitimately say that the Arabian sea was his, impregnably guarded from both sides and that no Mir Hussain could again challenge the right of Portugal. Half of Albuquerque's schemes had been completed, but the Bay of Bengal and the Eastern entrance remained. To these he turned his attention as soon as he had settled the affairs of Goa. In 1513 he set sail to the Eastern Seas in order to conquer Malacca and secure the entrance from that side. He had with him 18 ships carrying a thousand soldiers. The expedition was successful and Malacca was captured, fortified and made into the outer bastion of Portuguese power in the East. He opened negotiations with the King of Pegu who controlled the Arakan coast and established amicable relations with him.

With the conquest of Malacca and the establishment of friendly relations with the Ruler of Arakan, Albuquerque's oceanic strategy reached its completion. He had set out to build up a commercial Empire based on an unchallengeable position in the Indian Ocean. The coast line of Africa was already under Portuguese domination and what Albuquerque had to secure was a system of strong points which would cover the main areas. By the annexation of Socotra, by political suzerainty in Ormuz and by holding Malacca he established a system of control which remained unshaken as long as the Portuguese naval power remained powerful enough in Europe. To enable this policy to be carried out successfully it was essential that there should be a territorial base in India which could act as the central point of Portuguese power. The conquest and partial settlement of Goa and its development as a metropolitan city with the complete paraphernalia of government was therefore the foundation of all his schemes. In short Albuquerque's strategy may be summarised as (*a*) direct rule over Goa and its colonisation by mixed marriage, (*b*) fortresses and bases at strategic points, and (*c*) subordinate alliance with Rulers of coastal areas of strategic importance.

When Albuquerque's greatness is estimated it has to be remembered that these amazing results were achieved often in the face of the active opposition of his associate. Not only were the captains under him jealous of Albuquerque, but they carried on unceasing intrigue against him personally in India and at the Lisbon Court. The *Cartas* or Letters of Albuquerque show what extraordinary difficulties he had to overcome at every stage. Not only the insubordination of his subordinates and the lukewarm support of the King hampered his projects, but the complete chaos of the Portuguese financial administration in India was a source of perpetual trouble to him. Though an enormous revenue flowed into the Royal Treasury from the trade with India, Albuquerque himself had to complain that salaries of officers could not be paid for lack of funds. If in spite of all this he was able to achieve much, it must be attributed to the remarkable personality of the man who was never daunted by obstacles and whose unshakeable confidence in himself was based on the consciousness of outstanding superiority.

Albuquerque had no very high moral principles. He had no qualms about the means he used to achieve his ends and frankly confesses to have advised the heir-apparent of Calicut to poison the Zamorin who had foiled his plans and inflicted a heavy defeat on him. Though a fervent and devout Christian, he was not prevented by any humane considerations in massacring the Mussulmans at Goa and boasting about it to his equally devout master. Judged, however, by the standards of his time and of the Portuguese of his day, it may legitimately be claimed for Albuquerque that he was not only a great man, but a good and humane leader of men.

Though the commercial empire of Portugal declined with the decay of her political and naval power in Europe, following her union with Spain during the time of Philip II, Albuquerque's strategy has controlled the Indian Ocean since 1510. A glance at the map will show that it is on this foundation that Great Britain has built up not only her commercial but her continental Empire in the East. In that sense Albuquerque can justly be claimed as one of the prime architects of British Rule in India, no less than of the Portuguese dominion over the seas.

CHAPTER V

THE FIGHT FOR THE EMPIRE

The history of the Indian Ocean from 1515 to 1941 is a long commentary on the text elevated in the eighteenth century to the position of an axiom that the control of the Indian Ocean could best be secured by the control of the Atlantic. The rapid decline of Turkish naval power after the death of Khaireddin Barbarosa (the defeat at Lepanto only stopped his western advance) made any repetition of Mir Hussain's or Suleiman Pasha's intrusion into the Indian Ocean from the Red Sea side totally impossible. Naval power was monopolised by the Powers of the Atlantic and as long as the Portuguese position was unchallenged there, Albuquerque's structure of Empire could not be attacked. It was only when the overwhelming might of Philip II of Spain who had also become the King of Portugal suffered a heavy blow by the dispersal of the Armada and by the aggressive and organised piracy of Drake and the English captains that it became possible for other nations to sail into the Indian Seas from the Atlantic side.

The first to take advantage of the changed position were the Dutch. In 1592 at a meeting of the leading Dutch merchants at Amsterdam it was decided to found a Company for trading with India. In order to prepare for the voyage and for that purpose to collect the necessary information Cornelius de Houtman was sent to Lisbon. As the Kings of Spain still considered the Dutch to be their subjects, though rebellious and recalcitrant, Houtman did not experience any difficulty. But the most important source of information that the Dutch had at their disposal was provided by Jan Huygen Linchoten a noted traveller and writer. Linchoten came to India as Secretary to the Archibishop of Goa, a post which placed him in a position of advantage to study the strength and weakness of the Portuguese in India and to collect every kind of information.

He was one of the enthusiastic promoters of the Dutch Company.

In 1595 the first Dutch fleet, consisting of four vessels, commanded by Houtman set out for the East. From the commercial point of view it was a great success. The voyage opened the way for regular traffic and in 1604 a treaty was entered into between " the Zamorin the Emperor of Malabar " and Admiral S. Van der Hagen . . . . with a view to the expulsion of the Portuguese from the territory of His Highness and the rest of India." But the Dutch soon found that this was more easily promised than performed as long as the structure of Albuquerque endured. With the Portuguese firmly established at all the strategic centres of the Indian Ocean, there was no possibility whatever for the Dutch successfully to challenge Portuguese naval power. But the Hollanders soon discovered another way. They established their base outside the Indian Ocean at Batavia in the island of Java and slowly consolidated their position. Their first blow fell on Malacca which they captured in 1641, thereby opening the door from the East and shattering one of the main pillars of Albuquerque's structure. From Malacca, the next step was to attack Ceylon.

The importance of Ceylon had already been noted by the Dutch. Sebalt de Veert the Dutch Vice-Admiral reported to his Chief in April 1603 *" no place would be better for attacking the Portuguese (than Colombo) if we could only keep the King and the people of the country our friends." Boschower was even more emphatic. He declared " when they are once turned out of Ceylon they are out of India, as the island is the centre of India." Though some abortive attempts were made with this object, it was not until Dutch authority was established in the Straits of Malacca that the Hollanders were able to take effective action. The powerful Kings of Ceylon who were carrying on a relentless war against the Portuguese occupied one small post after another with the help of the Dutch, but all attempts against Colombo failed so long as the Dutch

* Pieris : Documents relating to Dutch Power in Ceylon.

were unable to bring a large naval force into the Indian seas. This became possible only after the occupation of Malacca. Van der Meyden after a long siege occupied Colombo on the 7th May, 1654. Without the support of Raja Simha, the King of Ceylon such a victory would not have been possible as the Dutch commanders themselves recognised.

With Malacca in their possession and with an advanced base in Colombo, it was not difficult for the Dutch to attack the minor establishments of the Portuguese on the Malabar coast. They soon began a campaign of harrying the Portuguese on the Arabian seas, often sailing up to Goa itself. In 1658, four years after the occupation of Colombo, Van Goens wrote: " we must be prepared to maintain our supremacy at sea. It is a pity our fleet generally reaches Goa too late. We should therefore propose that the next expedition leave Batavia about September 15th and sail direct to Ceylon " in order to enable an attack to be launched against Cochin.

Cochin along with the smaller settlements on the Malabar coast fell to the Dutch in 1663, but not without a desperate struggle. The Portuguese in their distress showed great heroism, but the Government at home was unequal to the task of maintaining a distant Empire. In a joint letter addressed to the King by Francis de Mello de Castro and Antonia de Countinho, they implored him. *" we feel it our bounden duty to acquaint you with the position of affairs in India and to inform you that unless we are properly assisted the whole of Your Majesty's possessions in India will be lost." The equipment of the fleet was borrowed from private individuals. " We earnestly implore Your Majesty to send us by next year adequate reinforcements, otherwise we shall not be able to resist the enemy at all." In short, the fall of the Portuguese oceanic power was not due to any fault in the system of defence, but to the breakdown of the machinery of the home government and the inability to maintain authority in the Atlantic.

Though the Dutch by holding the African coast, Ceylon and Malacca succeeded in a degree to the heritage of Albuquer-

* *Malabar and the Portuguese*, p. 157.

que, they had but little share in the shaping of policy in the Indian Ocean. The English and the French had followed in the Hollanders' wake and by the time the maritime power of the Portuguese disappeared from the Indian Ocean (1660-70) the Dutch had also, as a result of the rise of France and the fight with England, lost their position of primacy in the Atlantic. The interest from that time turns to the slow building up of British authority in the factory towns of Surat (and later Bombay), Madras and Calcutta and the cautious steps with which France moved towards an imperial policy in the East.

In the interval between the breakdown of Portuguese authority and the establishment of British supremacy Indian naval interests witnessed a remarkable revival. The Admirals of the Moghuls at Cambay and Janjira developed a naval power sufficiently strong to protect the commercial interests of the Empire. The great Malik Ambar was the founder of the Sidi naval power based on Janjira. When the power of the Deccan Sultanates waned and the Sidis had to withstand the attacks of Sivaji, they offered their allegiance to the Moghuls (1670) and Aurangazeb gladly accepted it. The Moghul navy in Surat which never counted for much joined the Sidis of Janjira who from that time, till the rise of British naval power in Bombay, were a major power on the West Coast and played a notable part in naval history.

The strength of the Moghul naval power and Sivaji's own failure to reduce Janjira, led the Maratha King to consider the question of creating a fleet for himself. Though bases were constructed and fleets built Sivaji's own efforts to command the sea met with only a moderate measure of success. The power of the Sidis after they had secured the support of Aurangazeb had grown greatly and they were able to command the sea from Goa to Gujerat. It was this mastery of the Konkan coast that saved the Moghul power in the South during the life time of Sivaji, and again it was the same naval support that enabled Aurangazeb to undertake his last great campaign.

The power of the Sidis on the Konkan coast was practically unchallenged till 1683. In that year Sidhoji Gujar the Maratha

Admiral took Suwarnadoorg and Vijayadoorg (Gheria) two important bases on the coast. Sidhoji who died soon afterwards, was succeeded in his post as Sarkhel or Admiral by Kanhoji Angre, a name that was to become famous in the naval annals of the Indian Ocean. Kanhoji was descended from a naval family, his own father Tukoji having served in Sivaji's fleet. Kanhoji himself joined the navy early in life and had displayed unusual ability in his career. He had captured Colaba, that vital promontory, from the Sidis, and had gradually recovered much of the sea board. His power grew without much support from the Central Government at Satara which was torn by dissensions, but when the Maratha Empire was reorganised under Balaji I, Kanhoji Angre who was supported by the great Minister, was able to direct the naval policy of the Empire and start on a career of active mastery of the Konkan seas.

His first act was to fortify his base. Vijayadoorg, or as it is better known in British naval history, Gheria, is at the mouth of a small river, which flows west from the Ghats but before falling into the sea takes a sharp turn to the north. A amall and narrow peninsula is thus formed, more like a tongue. The river runs parallel to the sea and the mouth forms a haven. The projection of land is itself a ridge, so that apart from the defensive strength of the fortress built on it, the ships moored in the river were concealed from the open sea. The heavier ships of the European nations even if they chased the Maratha fleet could not follow them up the river.

The natural strength of Gheria was such that it had been a bone of contention between the Sidis and the Marathas. As soon as it came into the possession of Kanhoji, he built a powerful citadel on the ridge which commanded the entrance to the river mouth. A specially selected garrison was stationed there and the fortress was armed and provisioned to withstand both attack and blockade. Behind the citadel on the river front were situated Kanhoji's dockyards. He engaged artisans, craftsmen, ship-builders and gun casters and settled them in the town that developed behind his fortress.

Thus equipped he was in a position to build better and stronger vessels, increase the efficiency of his equipment and the training of his men. In due course he was able to move forward and establish subsidiary anchorages, observation posts and bases all along the Konkan coast.

Soon the Sidis, the Portuguese and the British realised that a new power had arisen on the sea. The Sidis were the first to feel the weight of Angria's power. The fleet of the Moghul captains soon disappeared from the sea. The Portuguese had fallen into the position of a minor power and had neither the ships nor the men to challenge Kanhoji. It is when he turned to the British that he met with serious opposition.

When the Bombay Council realised the menace, they began a system of convoying their ships. They built corvettes for the purpose and it is interesting to note that the Bombay Marine which in due time evolved into the Royal Indian Navy had its origin in these corvettes which acted as escorts to the merchantmen of the Company for protection against Angria's power. The system of convoy did not frighten Kanhoji. It only led to a continuous naval warfare.

From Khanderi, his island base only 16 miles outside the Bombay harbour, the Maratha admiral levied a " Chauth " on the sea (" Chauth " or one-fourth was the Maratha tax on the territories they conquered). Angre claimed that in the territorial waters of the Marathas all who sailed without his permit should pay " Chauth". This conflicted with the British system of permits, an early forerunner of the Navicerts of today, inherited from the time of Cabral and Almeida. Angre opened the hostilities with the capture of an escorted yacht carrying the Governor of a factory. To put Angre down became the major preoccupation of the Bombay Council. Charles Boone the Governor of Bombay equipped a fleet, put Bombay in a defensive position with heavy artillery mounted on all walls, and then proceeded to attack Gheria (1717).* The expedition was led by Captain Barleu. The frigates which were heavily armed opened fire on Angre's fortifications,

* Downing, *History of India Wars.*

with however only negligible results. Foiled in this attempt a landing was effected some distance to the south of the Fort with the idea of attacking it from the land side; but under the heavy fire of the guns from the Fort the party had to retreat with severe loss. Boone's attempt thus ended in failure.

The Governor, however, was not a man to give up easily. The next year he again fitted out an expedition, this time with the more modest object of reducing Khanderi which was a perpetual menace to Bombay itself. A squadron of three ships had arrived from England carrying 300 European soldiers. This together with the Bombay fleet, and an army numbering no less than 2,500 was the powerful force which Boone sent out to reduce the island fortress. On November 5th 1718, the fleet opened fire, silencing many of the Maratha guns. By the evening the hopes of the attackers ran high, and it was decided to land at dawn. When actually the landing was attempted the Maratha guns mowed the party down. Only a very few survived the attempt. The British fleet then withdrew.

The Court of Directors, on hearing of this disaster, and fully realising what it meant, petitioned the King for naval help. The Government of the time was persuaded to send out a squadron of the Royal Navy consisting of four men-of-war under an officer of experience named Commodore Mathews. They arrived in Bombay in October 1722, and the most elaborate preparations were made to reduce once and for all time the menace of a rival naval power on the Konkan coast. The support of the Portuguese was also invited, and the Viceroy of Goa placed a contingent under his 'General of the North' to co-operate with the British forces. A powerful force of 5,000 men with 24 field guns supported the units of the Royal Navy. But for all this display of might, the attack on Kolaba ended in an inglorious failure. The Portuguese fled on attack; the English lost most of their guns and all their ammunition. Boone and Mathews retreated to the safety of Bombay.

After this victory against the combined forces of the English and the Portuguese, Kanhoji's power on the Konkan coast was unchallenged. But the Dutch who had not yet come into conflict with the Marathas felt that their dignity had been injured when Kanhoji captured two of their ships. They sent out from Holland a fleet of no less than 7 warships, two bomb vessels and a body of regular troops to attack Gheria (1724). The fate that met the Portuguese and the English awaited them also. The successors of de Ruyter retired after an ineffective demonstration. *" Victorious alike over the English, the Dutch and the Portuguese " the Maratha admiral, as an English historian declares, " sailed the Arabian sea in triumph".

Kanhoji's tactics were the same as those of Kunjali 150 years earlier. He operated with large numbers of light craft which were specially built for their speed. They were the equivalents of the Maratha pony which had made the name of the Deccan cultivators a terror to the Moghul armies. Lightly but adequately equipped they operated like wasps, surrounded heavier vessels and attacked them at close quarters. Their manoeuverability and speed made it impossible for the heavily armed ocean going East India men to deal with them effectively. The Gulivats of the Maratha admiral have been described by an authority as " lateen rigged craft of moderate dimensions, resembling a Sicilian felucca, fast and hardy under oars or sail, but an indifferent sea boat in heavy weather."

Kanhoji, who had this unique distinction of maintaining his naval power against England, Holland and Portugal and who with Kunjali III may well claim to be the greatest naval hero of India passed away in 1729. His son Sekhoji who was invested as admiral of the Maratha fleet was an equally intrepid commander. In 1738 the Dutch again tried to cow down the Angria but were repulsed. In 1749 Toolaji fought off the British man-of-war *Restoration.* At that time the Maratha Navy was supreme from Cutch to Cochin.

The position had become too serious for the British to take it lightly. After the siege of Arcot the Company had become a land power and unless the naval power of the Marathas was effectively dealt with, it might become a serious menace.

* Kincaid, *History of the Maratha People*, p. 240.

A powerful expedition was therefore sent out under Admiral Watson. A strong military force of 1,400 men under Colonel Clive, whose defence of Arcot had earned him a great reputation, arrived before Gheria. This force besieged the fortress, while the heavy guns from the ships bombarded it from the sea. After a two days battle Toolaji surrendered. The British ships had already forced the entrance into the river. The power of the Angrias on the sea was thus destroyed for ever.

Though Kanhoji and his successors were able to resist all attacks and to some extent even carry the war into the enemy's waters for a considerable time, the limitations of the Maratha naval power, as indeed of the Zamorin at an earlier date should be clearly recognised. Their authority was in what may be called the territorial waters. They had no oceanic policy: their ships were unable to meet the enemy out in the high seas. In fact the absence of islands and suitable bases covering the Indian coast made an oceanic policy difficult for them. Socotra was too far away and could not be defended except by a major naval power. Mauritius was over 2,500 miles away from the Konkan coast. For their strength the Indian navies had to depend on their coastal bases. The oceanic supremacy of Britain or Holland could not therefore be challenged either by Angrias or by Kunjalis. Their field of operation was restricted. But a new power capable of challenging this supremacy had entered the Indian Ocean, and to the great struggle that followed La Bourdannais' arrival in Eastern waters we must now turn our attention.

The French had appeared on the Malabar coast as early as 1527, but regular trade with India started only in 1601. The importance of keeping up with the other leading European States in the Indian Ocean was recognised by Henry IV who tried to establish a French East India Company on the model of the Dutch and English Companies. It is significant in view of later developments to note that the first regular authority from the French monarchy for trading in the Indian Ocean was in respect of Madagascar and the neighbouring islands. In

Madagascar itself they established Fort Dauphin as a convenient port of call.

The importance of Madagascar as a port in the Indian Ocean was emphasised in the report of Augustin de Beaulieu who stated, " I find the island proper, once we are established there for adventures to any place whatever in the East Indies." Various exploratory voyages were made but it was ouly in the time of Colbert who was anxious to establish the maritime greatness of France that the French East India Company was actually incorporated. The Company when constituted (1664) was given the perpetual grant of Madagascar and the neighbouring islands, In time factories were established and the French like other European nations had their small trade settlements in India.

The original idea of Colbert was to establish French authority in Ceylon and a considerable fleet under Jacob de la Haye set out for that purpose to India in March 1670. The Dutch who had only recently established themselves in Ceylon were, however, alert, and their fleet at Colombo was commanded by *Riycklof Van Goens, a naval officer of outstanding ability. De la Haye against his own judgment evaded action against the Dutch fleet when it was sighted and called at Candy. The King of Candy gave him the right to occupy the great harbour of Trincomalee and if De la Haye could have taken possession of it, the history of India might well have been different. But when he arrived at Trincomalee he discovered that the Dutch had been in secure possession of the harbour for some years. The only result of this expedition was the foundation of Pondichery by François Martin, who with six others had been left behind.

After the failure of this expedition French naval activity in the Indian Ocean was limited, though the frequent appearance of French vessels kept up the prestige of the factory at Pondichery. It was, however, only in the forties of the eighteenth century that the situation began to take a different turn. In 1735 Mahé La Bourdannais was appointed Governor

* For Van Goens see *Dutch in Malabar*.

of Mauritius which had been occupied a few years earlier. La Bourdonnais was a man of genius. He soon converted Mauritius into a strong naval base and slowly built up a fleet. In 1740 he arrived in the Bay of Bengal intending to intercept English merchantmen and generally attack British trade. After a cruise in the Bay in which he did some damage, la Bourdonniais returned to his base as England and France were at peace at that time. In 1744 the War of Austrian Succession broke out in Europe, disclosing at the same time a fundamental conflict between the French and English interests in South India. The French Governor at Pondichery, Dupleix had developed the ambition of making the French Company the masters of South India. Grandiose in his conceptions, and gifted with considerable political ability, Dupleix was a man who had no idea of naval power, the one essential factor in any scheme of European dominion in India. He was at home in decadent Indian Courts, was steeped in their intrigue and he affected the style and title of Nawab. Misled, as he was, by the ease with which he was able to establish political influence in these Courts and having recognised early that an efficient instrument for land warfare could be created out of Indian soldiers Dupleix set out to build his French Empire in India. But his scheme was doomed to failure from the beginning as the structure which Dupleix desired to raise lacked the foundation of naval support. Nor could he understand its importance.

When the Austrian War of Succession broke out La Bourdannais was back in Mauritius. There he received a summons from Dupleix to come out to the Bay of Bengal with the squadron at his command. This action of the French Governor was not so much with a view to secure the command of the sea or the destruction of the British fleet, but to give him support in his designs. La Bourdannais did not have a battle fleet with him, but he improvised one with the Company's ships lying in the harbour, and arrived in Indian waters in June 1746. The British fleet under Captain Peyton met him and in the action that ensued the French Commander had the advantage. Peyton and La Bourdannais met again in August when the English fleet declined engagement and left in haste for the safety of Hooghly. La Bourdannais was now free to act. He appeared before Madras and laid siege to it. After a show of resistance the Fort surrendered.

The fate of Britain's future empire in India hung in the balance. It should be remembered that Madras was then the major establishment of the English in India. The power of the Marathas gave no opportunity to Bombay to develop. Calcutta was no more than a marshy village, and till the death of the Moghul Garrnor Ali Verdi Khan in 1756, the British establishment in Bengal had hardly any political importance. On the other hand, Fort St. George was not only the most flourishing, but in view of the events in the Carnatic, politically the most important establishment in the East. It was by political intervention in Arcot, based on Madras that the foundation of the Empire had been laid many years before the battle of Plassey. If La Bourdannais' success could have been exploited and the English evicted permanently from the coast, the history of India might have been different. But Dupleix spinning his cobwebs and chasing the mirage of an Empire on land without an adequate realisation of naval strategy was not the man for it. The quarrels between La Bourdannais and Dupleix transformed what might have been a decisive event into a minor incident.

With the departure of La Bourdannais the command of the sea was again left to the English. Dupleix felt its effects immediately, for in spite of all his efforts he was not able to reduce from land the small British establishment of Fort St. David, only a few miles from Pondichery. The appearance of Boscawen's fleet consisting of six ships of the line, besides numerous smaller craft in the Indian waters a year later (1748) drove the lesson home, for it was Pondichery that was now besieged. Though the siege itself was unsuccessful, the mere assertion of naval supremacy was an important fact in deciding the future development of events. Dupleix's grandiose schemes vanished into thin air. His plans were all laid on the good old French tradition of besieging and taking towns and marching up and down. Against the country powers this was no doubt effective, but as long as Madras could be reinforced whenever needed and men and material poured into Fort St. George, Dupleix's continental plans, whatever immediate glamour they might add to his name, had not any chance of lasting success.

The next 30 years saw the firm establishment of British rule on the lands adjacent to the sea board in Madras and Bengal. The sea was firmly held during the time, though a French squadron under D'Aché arrived in Madras waters in 1758 to support the operations of Comte de Lally. In the actions that followed the British admiral Pocock was not able to gain any decisive advantage and D'Aché both landed his troops and gave support to Lally in military operations. But without a naval base nearer than Mauritius, it was impossible for the French commander to keep his fleet on the sea, and he had at a crucial time in the land campaign to withdraw to his base to recondition his ships. By the time of the next naval round, England had already *acquired an Empire in India* and become a major land power, but depending on the mastery of the sea for the sources of her strength. Her resources on the land both in Bengal and Madras were great. Powerful armies had been organised and Indian Rulers made to pay for them. Consequently, unless Britain permanently lost her command of the seas, there was no possibility of her Empire in India being seriously in danger. This essential fact has to be kept in mind in considering the Suffren interlude.

The next round opened in 1781 with the French Fleet under the Comte d'Orves, but he was soon joined by de Suffren who is justly recognised as a naval genius who takes his place with the great captains of all time, with Khaireddin, de Ruyter and Nelson. Opposing him was Sir Edward Hughes, a stolid commander, with sufficient experience, who, but for the misfortune which brought against him a man of transcendent genius, might have secured an honourable place in the annals of the British Navy.

Often there appear on the stage of history, like comets in the sky, men whose outstanding genius lights up brilliantly events of the time, shed an unnatural glow on men and affairs, and after a short spell disappear without leaving any noticeable trace in the steady march of time. Others less gifted and in many cases ordinary men, without either vision or the realisation of what they are doing, may set in motion events which revolutionise the course of history. If Vasco da Gama was an instance of the latter type, the Bailee de Suffren was the outstanding example of the former. Like a comet he arrived on the Indian scene. After a short period of three years, when he dominated the affairs of the Indian Ocean, he disappeared, leaving hardly a trace in the history of India.

Pierre André de Suffren Saint Tropez was one of the French officers for whom the maritime activity of France had not provided sufficient opportunity for distinction. During the revived activity of the French navy under the inspiration of Due de Choiseul he saw a great deal of action and achieved much distinction. Twice a prisoner in British hands, he developed a feeling of hostility towards the mistress of the seas, and finding that the French navy did not offer him sufficient opportunity, joined the Templars of Malta as a commander of their forces.* When war with Britain broke out following the declaration of American independence, he was recalled to service and given command of the fleet which was to attack the British on the Indian seas.

On his way out he attacked a British squadron sailing to the Indian waters and dispersed it off Lagos. Though the action was in no sense decisive it had the effect of preventing reinforcements from reaching Hughes, the British admiral, when the French fleet was ready for action against him.

On arriving in Indian waters Suffren found that the command of the fleet was in the hands of the Comte D' Orves, an officer whose abilities were in no way proportionate to his

* The title of Bailee by which he is known was awarded to him by the Knights of Malta, and seems to have been sent to him while he was in Indian waters.

high rank. Fortunately, however, D' Orves died in 1782 and Suffren succeeded to the command.

Then began a round of fights. In strength of ships-of-the-line and of fire power the navies were fairly equally matched. The British navy, however, had the great advantage of suitable naval bases on the coast, while the French had none. Another great handicap that the French commander suffered was the lack of training and discipline of his officers. Time after time orders were not carried out, and sometimes they were deliberately disobeyed. Though in some flagrant cases officers were punished and sent back to France, the lack of discipline was so general that Suffren had to make the best of it. It is interesting to remember that the great admiral died in a duel with the Prince de Mirpoix, who challenged Suffren for having insulted his princely dignity by sending back to France one of his relations as a punishment.

Suffren had another and greater difficulty. He had to keep cruising in such a way as to prevent reinforcements from reaching Hughes from the west. Unless Trincomalee on the Ceylon coast could be occupied and a base established there, the danger of Hughes receiving additional strength would always be present.

The engagements which Suffren fought in the Madras waters, though brilliant from the point of view of naval strategy, were indecisive, mainly through the insubordination of his officers. His own despatches to the Ministry of Marine in France, in themselves models of dispassionate reporting, show that Suffren did not for one moment forget that the primary object of all naval action is the destruction of the enemy fleet. Every time he fought Hughes he came near to it, but never succeeded in his attempt because his subordinates failed to act according to his orders.

Though thus foiled in his attempt to destroy his opponent's fleet, Suffren was able to wrest the mastery of the seas and carry out his immediate objects. He was able to keep Hughes away, to land forces in support of Hyder Ali's campaign in the Carnatic, and as a crowning achievement to capture Trincomalee (31st August, 1782), the great harbour from which the Bay of Bengal could be controlled and the communications with the west effectively cut.

Considering the resources at his disposal and the difficulties under which he worked, Suffren's achievement was indeed remarkable and fully justifies the judgment of his contemporaries and of the historians, including Mahan, that in all he was the outstanding genius which illumines French naval history.

Suffren's success, though notable as a personal triumph, had no historical significance, as it was thirty years too late. In the Carnatic campaigns, the English were in a position to depend on their own strength, at least after the death of Hyder Ali. After this short interlude (1782-84), which only served to emphasise the importance of a continuous maintenance of the supremacy of the sea for the control of events in India, and a warning for the future, British authority in the Indian seas was never again questioned till 1941.

The Napoleonic wars only witnessed the completion of the structure of Britain's naval Empire. Taking advantage of Napoleon's annexation of Holland, Britain was able to put into effect Albuquerque's policy in its entirety. Ceylon was conquered and annexed. The Dutch settlement at the Cape was taken over. The French possessions in the Indian Ocean which were at all times only hostages left in the hands of England, were conquered. Especially the island of Mauritius, from which La Bourdannais had sailed, for his conquest of Madras was not forgotten. It was annexed and became a part of the Empire.

In many ways the most important acquisition was Malacca, which was exchanged for the posts in Sumatra which Britain had conquered during the Napoleonic wars. Malacca had been from the days of the Hindu sovereignty of the sea considered the most strategic point for the control of the Straits. The Hindu kings had long ago recognised this. So had Albuquerque and the Dutch after them. Sir Stafford Raffles who had conquered Java and taken Batavia during the

Napoleonic wars, also occupied Malacca. Soon he realised that while Malacca was important for the control of the Bay of Bengal, the key of the Straits was in Singapore, which in 1824 he acquired from the Sultan of Johore. There he founded a modern city which in time became an important control point. That may be said to have put the coping-stone on the edifice of British supremacy in the Indian Ocean. Thus the strategy of Albuquerque found its culmination and Britain the sole power in the Indian Ocean since the Treaty of Vienna, with her authority firmly established at all strategic points and an Empire in India created on these pillars in the sea, ruled the Indian Ocean as a British lake.

CHAPTER VI

THE BRITISH LAKE

In the nineteenth century, after the French fleet was annihilated at Trafalgar in 1805, Great Britain was the only naval power in the world. It was the century in which it could legitimately be said that Britannia ruled the waves. The mere presence of a British gunboat anywhere in the seven seas had decisive effects both for maintenance of peace and enforcement of policy. The White House was burnt down by a British raiding party. British naval support secured the independence of South America. All along the coasts of China and even in her inland rivers British warships proclaimed the might of Neptune. So far as the Indian Ocean was concerned, it was, even more than all other Oceanic areas, a British lake. No European nation had any interest in that vast oceanic surface, nor in the lands adjacent to it.

The one development in the nineteenth century which affected the Indian Ocean, the construction of the Suez Canal, only strengthened British hold on the seas. With her unchallenged supremacy in the Mediterranean, and with the acquisition of authority over Egypt and the annexation of Cyprus, the Mediterranean route to India became a private subway for Britain, with controls at different stages—Gibraltar, Malta, Port Said and Aden. The Red Sea became an exclusively British sea lane, bolted and barred at both entrances. Aden assumed the importance it possessed during the time of Egyptian and Arabian navigation in the Indian Ocean, and it may well be said that the Suez Canal became, as events developed, the strongest link in the chain which bound India to Britain.

The construction of the Canal had also other effects. It restored the importance of the traditional Red Sea Route to Europe. That had been the famous highway over which practically the entire trade of India with Europe had passed till

Vasco da Gama arrived at Calicut and opened up the Cape route. The Turkish control of the narrow isthmus and the vital Egyptian littoral had practically cut off India's connection with the west, except through the round-about African route. With the opening of the Canal, India and the Indian Ocean became many thousands mile nearer to the European bases of power and consequently, along with an unprecedented development of trade, it also witnessed more effective control of the Indian Ocean routes.

It was not, and perhaps could not have been foreseen at the time that the opening of this route will once again arouse the cupidity of Venice or her modern successors. The Mediterranean nations, especially reunited Italy, began to cast longing eyes towards the Indian trade which had once been the monopoly of Venice. But the developments of that cupidity were still in the womb of Time, as the control of Egypt and the Canal gave to Britain an additional strength in the Indian Ocean which further secured her against intruders from the West.

The *fin de siècle*, however, saw the tentative beginnings of a new situation. In the Far East, America, by defeating Spain, occupied the Philippines in 1895, thus entering the Pacific Ocean as at least a potentially major naval power. Almost at the same time Japan, after defeating China in a naval engagement, took the first ominous step towards her southward expansion by the annexation of Formosa. These opening moves in the vast chess-board of the Pacific passed unnoticed in their effects on the Indian Ocean. The axiom of the previous three centuries that the control of the Indian Ocean was a corollary to the mastery of the Atlantic was being definitely challenged as events proved, though this aspect of the question was entirely ignored at the time.

In the Indian Ocean itself there were signs of a change. Since the occupation of Mauritius during the wars of the French Revolution, France had no position in the Indian Ocean. The occupation of Madagascar in the 'nineties gave to her a large territorial interest, and a base of great natural strength in Diego Suarez, which could in case of a breakdown of the naval power based on India, control the main routes of the Indian Ocean. This, it will be remembered, was the argument which led the United Nations to take action against Vichy authorities and deprive Japan of a possible base on that side.

Almost simultaneously Germany also entered the Indian Ocean. She occupied Tanganyka, which gave her a coast-line on the Ocean. She claimed a protectorate over Zanzibar, obviously with the object of developing it as a naval base. Its exchange with Heligoland did not seriously alter the German position, as the extensive territories of German East Africa, when developed, would have made her, in view of her increasing maritime activity, a major naval power in the Indian Ocean. Nor was Italy to be denied her place. By occupying Somaliland, which gave her a seaboard on the Indian Ocean, she also put in her claim for whatever the future may unfold.

In the Red Sea also, international rivalry had begun to show itself. France established herself at Jibuti, just across Aden. Italy developed the Colony of Eritrea and began examining the possibilities of developing a naval base at Massawa, in itself a fine harbour of great natural strength. She also claimed political interests in the territory of Yemen on the Arabian side of the Red Sea, thereby threatening the safety of the vital British centre of Aden. The Red Sea also entered into the calculations of German world strategy. Imperial Germany knew well enough that entry into the Indian Ocean from the side of the Atlantic was not possible for her, not only because of Britain's overwhelming naval might, but also because of the geographical position of the British Isles blocking her entry into the Atlantic Ocean. Colonial possessions on the African littoral of the Indian Ocean gave her no definite advantage against Britain. She had to reach the Indian Ocean through another route.

Not being a Mediterranean power, and with no chance of entering the Red Sea, which in any case was secured and controlled by Britain, Germany under William II evolved the gradiose scheme of a direct entry from the side of land into the

Persian Gulf. This was to connect Berlin with Baghdad by a direct rail route. The Berlin-Baghdad Railway was indeed a great conception. It was historically a reply to Vasco da Gama's achievement; the attempt of the land power to outflank the sea. It short-circuited both the Atlantic and the Mediterranean and gave entry into the Indian Ocean in a manner which could set at nought the carefully planned chain of naval bases, fuelling stations and political authority which had come into existence since the time of Albuquerque. The Persian Gulf had not played a part in the history of the Indian Ocean after Bin Kassim led his seaborne forces into Sind. The Berlin-Baghdad Railway would have enabled it to regain the importance it had lost and provided Germany with a safe back-door entrance into the Indian Ocean.

The Mesopotamian valley, watered by the Tigris and the Euphrates, has been a strategic centre in Asiatic history. From the earliest times it had been the seat of powerful Empires. The imperial power of Nineveh and Babylon had influenced the Indian Ocean in the earlier days, and the Khalifs of Baghdad had encouraged the great merchant sailors whose fleets sailed out from Basra and covered the Indian Ocean for many centuries. Intrinsically there was nothing unsound in the idea of establishing a naval base on the Persian Gulf.

But in the circumstances of the time the scheme was incapable of effective fulfilment. The immediate hinterland was in an extremely backward state. No doubt German engineering skill would have built the railway and established a direct land route, but the conversion of the Persian Gulf into a protected naval area from which the mastery of the Indian Ocean could be challenged was utterly impossible for a power like Germany whose industrial strength was situated thousands of miles away and whose communications with Baghdad had to pass through the territories of other industrially backward States.

Further, the Turkish Empire under the later Sultans was in no position to carry out a scheme of that nature; and it was too decayed and decrepit in its administrative machinery to enable the German allies to work through it. From the most prosperous territory of the Empire the hinterland of the Persian Gulf had become one of the most backward. Its resources were unexploited; its agriculture had decayed; it had no industry worth speaking of. In those circumstances the Berlin-Baghdad Railway, even if it had led to the establishment of a naval base in Basra, could not have menaced the defences of India. At best it would have been a defensive measure protecting the flank of Turkey. The attack on Mesopotamia, undertaken across the sea from bases in India could no doubt have been effectively prevented, if the scheme had materialised. But aggressive action to challenge the mastery of the sea would have been impossible. German submarines could have crept into the Indian Ocean, harassed the trade of India like the pirates of old, but to achieve anything more than that a complete reorganisation of the hinterland would have been necessary.

The picture that the Indian Ocean presented in the period immediately before the Great War of 1914-18 was something like the following. Great Britain sailed the seas of the Indian Ocean as an absolute mistress. Her power was overwhelming at every point, and no nation or combination of nations could have contested her authority in the slightest degree. But it was clear that the storms were gathering. The major European nations had acquired interests in the Indian Ocean area. France, Germany and Italy had territories on the African coast and the names of Diego Suarez, Jibuti, Massawa and Mogadaccio were coming into prominence. Germany, a prisoner in the Baltic, was developing schemes for a land route which would give her an independent entry into the Arabian Sea.

The war of 1914-18 eliminated Germany from the Indian Ocean. The establishment of the independent State of Iraq and the acquisition of interests in that country in the form of the Mosul oilfield were the replies, then considered adequate, to a threat to the Indian Ocean from the side of the Persian Gulf. But the tendencies that were apparent before 1914 became only more pronounced in the interlude between the two wars. At enormous cost, France developed Diego Saurez into a powerful naval base. Her object in doing so was in no way concealed from the world. The French Minister of Marine declared in the Chamber of Deputies that the naval base, if properly developed, will command the Indian Ocean. Fascist Italy was not to be outdone. Mussolini had made up his mind that the future of Italy lay on the sea, Massawa on the Red Sea coast was converted into a great naval base, and it was the boast of the Duce that he had cut the connection between India and Suez.

The acquisition of Abyssinia was also a part of this great scheme. With only the small hinterland of Eritrea, Massava could not be much of a danger. But with a large territory with undeveloped resources, and a climate in the higher altitudes suitable for European colonisation, an empire could be established on the mainland of Africa which could be held and defended independently, even if communications were cut off with Italy. With a growing European population and a trained native army, Abyssinia and Eritrea could meet any challenge coming from the sea. Besides, with the strength that such an empire can develop, Massawa will cease to be merely a naval station but a great base from which the Red Sea can be controlled.

Between the Abyssinian Empire and the Italian colony on the Indian Ocean lay the small British colony of Somaliland, which it was not easy to defend. Italian Somaliland had Mogdishu as a port on the Indian Ocean, and if in case of war the intervening area could be conquered (as indeed it was) then the new Abyssinian Empire of Mussolini would not only have effectively cut the connection between the Mediterranean and India, but have entered the Indian Ocean as a considerable naval power. Her position in the Red Sea would have been impregnable. Aden would have not only been rendered useless for controlling the entrance, but itself menaced from the land side in view of the political relations established by Italy with Yemen which, with the consolidation of Italian power on the other side of the Red Sea, had taken a more definite shape. But the war came five years too soon for Mussolini. His schemes for converting Abyssinia and Eritrea into a great land empire were only half completed when the European War broke out.

It is nevertheless noteworthy that British Somaliland was occupied by the Italians in the first stage of the war, thus uniting the Red Sea empire with the Indian Ocean littoral. If the colonisation of Ethiopia by Italians had been completed and the local armies had been properly organised, no colonial war could have eliminated the danger to the Indian Ocean. As it was Massawa had to surrender when the land campaign broke the power of the Italians on the mainland, and the dream of dominating the Red Sea and controlling the Gulf of Aden disappeared with it.

Both France and Italy had forgotten the lessons of history. Colonies away from the Motherland, unless dependent on their own strength, are only hostages given to naval powers. The fate of the French colonies in the Napoleonic wars, of the Spanish islands in the Spanish-American war, and German colonies in the last war, demonstrated clearly that overseas colonies for nations who do not enjoy mastery of the seas are no more than hostages in the hands of the enemy. They constitute no great threat to anyone, and the British could afford to look on with amusement at feverish preparations at Massawa and on the development of Diego Suarez in the period before the Second Great War.

The interlude between the wars saw two important developments, one of which was spectacular and the other small enough to pass unnoticed. Following the denunciation of the Anglo-Japanese alliance, Britain decided to build a naval base at Singapore, meant to be the Gibraltar of the East. Japan objected to this proposal on the ground that the Washington Agreement had stipulated that no new base will be constructed in the Pacific by any one of the three signatories. But clearly the objection was invalid as Singapore was not in the Pacific. After much argument and some vacillation, the scheme was carried through. Singapore, with its floating docks, with its enormous guns mounted on specially designed platforms, with its dry docks and aerodromes, became the bastion in the East and the symbol of Britain's naval might. Barring the entry into the Indian Ocean, the great fortress was designed to withstand the attack of any combination of naval powers, and when the work was completed Britain was legitimately proud of the great fortress that had arisen as a warning and as a threat to anyone who dared to question the supremacy of Britain in the Indian Ocean.

The second event, which received no such publicity and hardly received any notice at all, was the creation of a small Royal Indian Navy. It was only an insignificant beginning, but historically a matter of the greatest significance. After the destruction of the Maratha naval power in 1751, Indians were sailing the seas for the first time in warships—small and insignificant units, no doubt, but symbolic of the resuscitation of the old forces which had for at least two millenia held the mastery of the Indian seas.

The developments in the Pacific were also of supreme significance in this period. Japan had, as a result of the Treaty of Versailles, acquired islands in the Middle Pacific originally held by Germany. The acrimonious discussions at the peace conference regarding the small island of Yap showed that Japan was looking southward, and that the lessons of geopolitics had been carefully learnt in Tokio. The development of Japanese bases at Truk and Yapa was indeed significant. No less significant was the attitude of the U.S.A. The acquisition of the Philippines had made her a major Pacific power. At Pearl Harbour she developed a first-class base, with a chain of important stations at Midway, Wake and Guam, terminating in the naval fortress of Corregidor. Her dominant interests in China gave to these naval arrangements a significance which was not lost on those whom Commodore Perry had rudely awakened from their mediæval slumber.

Another factor of significance to the Indian Ocean was the interest which Japan had begun to show in the Isthmus of Kra. After the decision to go forward with the Singapore plans, it came to be widely believed that Japan was negotiating with the Siam Government for the construction of a Canal across the Isthmus which would have affected the dominant position of Singapore, and given the navy of Japan a safe entry into the Indian Ocean. In 1934, the British Parliament discussed this question. Though Sir John Simon, the Foreign Secretary, denied the truth of the rumours, the statement of the Japanese Minister to Siam was that if the Canal was built, he saw no reason why it should interfere with Singapore. Though no Canal project seems to have come under active consideration, the mere fact of the question coming under discussion showed Japan's interest in a free access to the Indian Ocean.

The European war, leading imperceptibly into the war in the Pacific changed the entire situation in the Indian waters. After the fall of France, and Italian intervention in the Mediterranean and the Red Sea, Great Britain was in no position to make her voice effective in the Far East. Unheralded, Japan had moved south, occupied the island of Hainan opposite Tonkin, and established close relations with Siam. The vast coastal area of China up to Canton had already passed into her hands, and by December 1941, she had transformed not only the seas up to the mouth of the Mekong into an area of Japanese supremacy, but had developed her army into a vast continental power which could strike at any place in East Asia, provied the mastery of the Chinese sea was assured.

The destruction of the Pacific fleet at Pearl Harbour, and the sinking of the *Prince of Wales* and the *Repulse* effected a revolutionary change in the whole aspect of the Eastern Oceans. In a lightning campaign the combined forces of the Mikado occupied the Philippines, forced the surrender of Corrigedor, invaded and conquered the stretch of islands from Sumatra to New Guinea, and cut the American communications by taking Guam and Wake. In a campaign of less than 3 months the Peninsula of Malaya was occupied and Malacca taken. The *army* of Nippon stood on the Johore shores overlooking the great fortress of Singapore. The gateway to the Indian Ocean was attacked from the land side. After a short siege Singapore surrendered and the safety and security of the Indian Ocean, for 150 years a British lake, had vanished at one stroke.

The entry of Japan into the Indian Ocean demonstrated clearly the entire dependence of the security of India on the mastery of the seas. The Andamans and Nicobars passed into enemy hands. That sealed the doom of Burma, which was thereby cut off from all sea communications with India. The units of the fleet at Trincomalee were attacked and destroyed and as the Commander-in-Chief in India openly confessed a few months ago, there was nothing to stop Japan at that time from landing anywhere she pleased on the Indian coast line.

Nor was this all. In the critical months of April 1942, the fate of Ceylon hung in the balance. A Japanese battle fleet appeared in the Bay of Bengal, and the units of the British navy at Trincomalee went down to an aerial attack from carrier based planes. The timely appearance of the American fleet in the Coral Sea forced Japan to withdraw her fleet from the Indian waters, and Ceylon was thus saved from a sea-borne invasion. Though deprived of the fruits of their mastery of the Bay, Japanese submarines began to appear in the Arabian Sea and to take a heavy toll of mercantile shipping, Britain reacted with vigour by the immediate occupation of the French islands, especially of Madagascar, and the great naval base of Diego Suarez. Though the line of communication was thus safeguarded, the Arabian Sea could not be cleared of Japanese submarines, and the west as well as the east coast of India remains exposed to the depredations of the undersea craft.

Oceanic strategy has therefore entered into the consideration of the Indian question with a dramatic suddenness which could not have been foreseen before March 1942. The whole question of Indian defence, has, as a result, to be reconsidered, both in the light of history and of recent events. The era of protected sea communications has ended for India, and the question of the control of oceanic areas surrounding India stares us now in the face.

CHAPTER VII

CONCLUSION

The interests of India in the Indian Ocean are different from those of the other countries whose shores are washed by its waters. The other countries are not so entirely dependent as India on this Ocean. South Africa and Malaya are washed by the Atlantic and Pacific Oceans respectively. So far as the other African areas are concerned, they are mainly continental and have only one side touching the Ocean. The position of Arabia is also different. The Red Sea is well protected by the Straits of Bab el Mandeb, and the Isthmus of Suez, while the Canal provides an exit into the Mediterranean. Equally, the Persian Gulf is a naturally protected area. It is only the south east coast of Arabia which is washed by the Indian Ocean. But in respect of that coast, as well as the southern coast of Persia, the barren nature of the country provides the greatest measure of natural protection. It is also necessary to remember that, in view of the desert character of Arabia Felix and of the southern shores of Persia, no naval power has ever attempted to conquer those areas from the side of the sea.

The position is far different in the case of India. The peninsular character of the country with its extensive and open coast line, and with a littoral which is extemely fertile and rich in resources, makes India entirely dependent on the Indian Ocean. Her national interests have been mainly on the Indian Ocean over which her vast trade, has for the most part, found its way to the marts of the world all through history. Few historians have recognised this outstanding fact, for the reason that Indian histories so far have been written not from the point of view of India as a whole, but from the point of view of Delhi and its changing dynasties. The history of India which the European scholars wrote, was based on the records of Moslem chroniclers, whose point of view was practically Central Asian. So far as the Hindu period was concerned, it was reconstructed from inscriptions, coins and epigraphic records, which, by their very nature, were fragmentary and unrelated to each other. It is only during the last 20 years that any attempt has been made to understand the forces that operated to make India what it is.

A true appreciation of Indian historical forces will show beyond doubt, that whoever controls the Indian Ocean has India at his mercy. The authority that can be exercised over her long coast line, with the minimum of force makes the subjection perpetual, while invasion from across the land frontier has naturally to be sporadic. Besides, such an invasion by land must lead to an occupation by the invading force, which, owing to the size, population and retentive culture of the country ends in the conqueror becoming conquered in the course of a few generations. No two countries have been so often conquered from the land side as India and China. But in the case of both, such conquests, though they led to temporary convulsions, only ended in the assimilation of the conqueror in the general pattern of the local civilisation.

Control from the side of the sea is different. It operates as a stranglehold especially when, as in the case of India, as a result of geographical factors, the country's prosperity is dependent almost exclusively on sea trade. The history of the last three centuries has shown that any power which has unquestioned mastery of the sea and strength to sustain a land campaign can hold the Empire of India, monopolise her trade, and exploit her unlimited resources. The land routes out of India are few. In fact, even the North-western frontier, the one land lane of trade, provides but little facility for commerce. On the other hand, the sea routes available to India, from her ports from Karachi to Chittagong, take her easily to all parts of the world. For sea trade no country is so centrally situated. The Indian ports are practically equidistant from the great markets of Europe and the Far East, while Africa and the islands of the Pacific are equally accessible to her. This extremely strategic position has given to the commerce of India a world importance, which, as we have seen, has been one of the motivating factors of the past, leading to revolutionary political changes.

This is true more than ever at the present time. While to other countries, the Indian Ocean is only one of the important oceanic areas, to India it is the vital sea. Her life lines are concentrated in that area. Her future is dependent on the freedom of that vast water surface. No industrial development, no commercial growth, no stable political structure is possible for her unless the Indian Ocean is free and her own shores fully protected. The Indian Ocean must therefore remain truly Indian.

The bare facts of the present war have proved this beyond doubt. The strategic area in Indian warfare is not so much the Burmese frontier, as the neglected Andaman islands. What is of the utmost importance in safeguarding India's communication with Europe is not Bombay or Colombo, but Diego Suarez. It is the oceanic space that dominates the strategy of Indian defence.

It may be emphasised that her claim to interests in the Indian Ocean is not with a view to any aggression or imperialist design, but purely and solely as a matter of defence. India cannot exist without the Indian Ocean being free. From the nature of the territories washed by the Indian Ocean (except Malaya) it is clear that India will be in no position to dominate them politically by naval strength. Neither Arabia, nor Persia can be affected by the control of the Ocean by India.

Apart from the questions of Indian defence and trade, both of which are entirely dependent on the Indian Ocean and the great sea routes which intersect its surface, India has also other interests. Large Indian settlements exist all along the African coast from the Cape of Good Hope to Kenya. Mauritius has an important and growing Indian population settled on that island now for two centuries. On the eastern side, in Singapore, Malaya and Burma there are important interests which cannot be overlooked. In fact Indian interests have extended to the different sides of this Oceanic area.

The strategic position has, however, considerably changed from the palmy days of the ninteenth century. It is not only the Atlantic that now counts in naval affairs. The growth of two powerful naval powers in the Pacific has revolutionised the basic assumptions of the earlier centuries regarding naval supremacy in the Indian Ocean. Japan's lightning conquest of Singapore and her consequent control of the Bay of Bengal from the bases at Malacca and the Andamans and the harbours on the Burmese coast, have demonstrated that the challenge may come more easily from the East than from the West. The elimination of Japan from the ranks of naval powers will in no way solve the problem, for there is every reason to think that a victorious China will embark on a naval career. With her bases extending as far south as Hainan, China is placed in even a more advantageous position than Japan. Further, the entire southern region has large and powerful Chinese settlements and a southward expansion by land cannot be ruled out in the case of a resuscitated Chinese Republic.

That China does intend to embark on a policy of large scale naval expansion is clear enough from the attitude of both Chungking and Nangking. One of the claims which Chungking spokesmen put forward from time to time is that the Japanese Navy should be handed over to China after the war. So far as Nangking is concerned, that government has under Japanese inspiration already created a navy and is pushing forward a scheme of naval expansion. Arsenals, dockyards and academies are being established and a 'navy day' is celebrated officially to impress on the Chinese the importance of naval expansion.

Nor should it be forgotten that the Chinese have a long naval tradition. From the earliest times they have navigated the seas. So late as the fifteenth century Chinese fleets visited India. The fleet that sailed under Cheng Ho in 1405 and visited Calicut consisted of no less than 62 ships. In the period between 1405 and 1430 Chinese fleets visited Calicut no less than six times. It was only the existence of the naval power of the Sri Vijayas that prevented the Chinese from establishing their authority in the Indonesian Archipelego and as the Portuguese appeared soon after the breakdown of Sri Vijaya, the southward expansion of China over oceanic space was shut out. That movement towards the south which is indicated by the significant demography of the area may, and in all probability will, be reflected in the naval policy of resurgent China.

The strategic position of Indo-China should also not be forgotten in this connection. The French Colony covers the coast line from Tonkin to well inside the Gulf of Siam. This is an area of tension, in view of the breakdown of French authority in the East. If, as is possible, Indo-China falls after the war within the Chinese sphere of influence, her authority over the southern waters will clearly become dominant.

From the long period point of view, Japan will also have to be taken into consideration as a naval power. As an island power her interests are mainly on the sea, and unless a firm unity of purpose between not only her present enemies, but also between them and Russia for the purpose of keeping her permanently down is postulated, which in view of conflicting interests is inconceivable, Japan will again become a considerable naval power within a reasonable time.

The position of America in the Middle and Southern Pacific with her base at Pearl Harbour does not require any detailed discussion. But it may be noticed that powerful interests in the U.S.A. are urging on the administration that it is necessary to have many more island bases in order to ensure American naval preponderance in the Pacific. The naval power of the U.S.A. is alrady such as to make it a factor to be counted in any part of the " Indivisible Sea."

After the war, it is obvious that America will come back to Corrigedor. With a deeper appreciation of the strategic importance of the covered South China Sea—a true Mediterranean of the Pacific—she will be in a dominant position in that area, bearing directly on Singapore. The Islands of the Archipelago will be entirely at her mercy. What is perhaps even more important from the point of view of the Indian Ocean, is the possibility of direct access from the South.

The main field of American naval and air operations has been New Guinea, New Britain and other islands on the outer fringe of the Archipelago. American navalists fully realise the importance of these islands and if the U.S.A. acquires a base, say in Papua, her entry into the Indian Ocean will be free and unmolested.

America has developed considerable interests in the Middle East. Oil concessions in Saudi Arabia and in Iran, not to speak of the Bahrein islands indicate the growth of strong economic interests in the drainage area of the Indian Ocean. America will emerge out of the present war with global and not hemispheric ideas of strategy, and the possibility therefore has to be visualised of America entering the Indian Ocean as a major naval power.

Another eventuality has also to be faced. At least from the time of the Chaldeans the Persian Gulf has had a great influence on the Indian Ocean. It should not be forgotton that the first sea-borne invasion of India (or Sind) started from the Persian Gulf. Though since the fall of Baghdad Khalifs the Persian Gulf has not been the centre of a great naval power, the proposal of the Berlin-Baghdad Railway was a clear indication, as pointed out earlier, that land powers seeking entry into the Gulf may change the balance in the Arabian Sea. William II's scheme could, however, never have materialised in the naval sense without a mastery of the intervening area.

It may be considered that the establishment of Iraq as an independent State under a British guarantee has eliminated the possibility of a great land power stretching out its authority to the Persian Gulf. But the recent incident of Al Ghilani and the danger which threatened the whole Allied strategy as a result of that betrayal show that one may well be exaggerating the safety assured by such political arrangements. Besides, as against a considerable land power Iraq cannot defend herself even with British support, for before Britian could transport the necessary help, Iraq could be overrun by a rapid campaign such as we have often witnessed in the present war.

Also, though Germany has been eliminated, the threat may be revived from another quarter. The political, industrial and military organisation of Central Asia under the Soviets gives a new content to the old Russian conception of unrestricted entry into the open sea. Vladivostock as a base is essential for the defence of the Soviets in the Far East, but her developed hinterland is too far away to make it more than a naval base. Nor would an entry into the Aegean, for long the object of Russian policy, meet her changed industrial and commercial requirements. The important fact to be considered is the great and unprecedented development of Central Asia and obviously it will demand an outlet into the sea. The lines of traffic developed for the purposes of Lend Lease aid to Russia in the present war have demonstrated the vital importance of the Persian Gulf to the Soviets.* It is the

*Extract from "America's Strategy in World Politics" by N. J. Spykman.

Page 181—"Because of the inadequacy of the Arctic Coast as an outlet to the ocean, the great heartland can find access to the sea only by routes that cross the encircling mountain barrier and the border zone beyond. The only easy exits are through the Baltic and the Black Seas and by the overland routes through the North German plain between the Scandinavian massif and the Carpathians. The other passages are narrow and difficult, and limited to single roads over arduous mountain passes. Russian Turkestan can find an outlet only across the Kyhber Pass to the valley of the Indus. It has one other outlet to a distant ocean, the old silk route across the passes of the Tien Shan Mountains through Sinkiang north of Tibet to Central China and the Pacific. Central Siberia can reach the sea through the depression between the Tien Shah and the Altai Mountains over the Mongolian plateau to Peking and the Gulf of Chih-Li or north of the Altai ranges, around Lake Baikal, down the valley of the Amur to the Japanese Sea.

Page 182—"From Central Asia came the early invasions into the border zone, the irruptions of nomadic barbarians into Europe, Persia, India and China. Most persistent has been the pressure on Europe and China because geography forces the flow of power into the east-west channel. To the north lie tundra waste and the Polar Sea: to the south stretches a zone of barren desert and the highest mountain barrier in the world; in between an easy grassland belt provides an area of mobility. Along this broad way the ancient horsemen of the plains exerted pressure on Vienna and Peking, and along this same line have flowed the power thrusts of modern Russia. For two hundred years, since the time of Peter the Great, Russia has attempted to break through the encircling ring of border states and reach the ocean. Geography and sea power have persistently thwarted her."

uninterrupted supply of material into Basra and its transport across Persia into the Soviet territory that rendered the heroic defence of Russia possible. The lesson is not likely to be forgotten.

The possibility of the presence of a naval power of the magnitude, resources and persistance of Russia on the Persian Gulf is in itself sufficient to revolutionise the strategy in respect of the Indian Ocean. It should be remembered that ever since the Indian Ocean came into the vortex of world politics there was never any occasion when such a contingency arose to upset the calculation of Oceanic strategy. Sultan Suleiman the Magnificent, it is true, issued an Order to his Begler Beg in Egypt and Suleiman Pasha did in compliance with that Order arrive on the Indian waters. But a naval power based on Egypt could not act with any effect in the Indian Ocean, especially when the exit from the Red Sea was barred at the mouth. If the Turkish Sultans had not been tied to a barren European policy and if they had in furtherance of Suleiman's scheme developed a navy in the Persian Gulf, they could have seriously challenged European domination in the Indian Ocean. But the Turks were essentially a Mediterranean power and they neglected the Persian Gulf, both commercially and from the naval point of view. Besides, after Khaireddin Barbarosa the fortunes of the Turkish navy were on the decline and with the defeat of Ali Pasha at Lepanto it ceased to count as a serious instrument of warfare. As a result, no power with homelands on the Indian Ocean had so far been able to enter in this naval competition. If the Russians reach the Indian Ocean, it will therefore be the first time in a thousand years that a naval power entered the Ocean from that side.

The changes in naval strategy which such a possibility involves need not be touched upon here at any length. The only observation that need be made is that all the accepted formulae of Oceanic security in so far as they affect the Arabian sea will have to be examined afresh, especially in relation to the changes in the scope and range of air and underwater attack which the present war has brought to light. The enormous growth of the power of shore defences, the effectiveness of the attack of land based planes and other important factors have restricted the scope of naval action against bases and at the same time projected into the sea the strength of land powers. A strong military State on the Persian Gulf could make that an impregnable base and resist successfully all attacks from the sea. If that power is also industrially advanced and capable of constructing and maintaining on the sea large and powerful navies, then the Persian Gulf could become what Scapa Flow is to the Atlantic and Wilhelmshaven to the Baltic. The problem is of the utmost importance to the future of India.

From the battle of Salamis to that of the Straits of Tushima the command of the sea was secured by ranged battle. It was a question of ship against ship, of gun against gun. But the present three dimensional warfare in the sea creates a completely new set of problems. It is the action of torpedo carrying aircraft at Taranto Bay that put a large portion of the Italian navy out of the war against Britain. Again at Pearl Harbour and off Kotabharu, it was aircraft action that decided the command of the sea for the time being. In fact, in this war only two battles of any significance have taken place on the sea between warships in regular battle line. The first was the battle of the Java seas in which Admiral Helfrich attempted in vain to emulate the tactics of de Ruyter. The other was off Cape Matapan where the naval forces met in open combat. In both cases, however, the engagement was three dimensional, not only ship against ship, but with submarine and aircraft.

In regard to the Indian Ocean these facts have very considerable significance. With no covering islands from which aircraft can act, the bases on the open coast line of India can be bombed from aircraft carriers, as Japanese action against Trincomalee and Colombo has shown us. It is true that the absence of islands operates as a protection against land based aircraft, but obviously with the great length of the peninsular coast line, it is not possible to have air bases sufficient to afford protection at every point. Unless, therefore, distant bases like Singapore, Mauritius, Aden and Socotra are firmly held and the naval air arm developed in order to afford sufficient protection to these posts, there will be no security or safety for India.

A further fact which has to be considered in regard to the future of naval power in the Indian Ocean is the distribution of fuel. A navy can only operate within the range of its fuel supply and in times of war independent sources of fuel are essential for the maintenance of supremacy on the sea. Even the largest and most efficient fleet will not be in a position to operate unless the necessary fuel is available. The Indian Ocean area has adequate sources of oil supply, but they lie outside the geographical limits of India. In Persia, Iraq and Bahrein liquid fuel is abundant. So it is on the eastern side of the Ocean, in Burma and in Sumatra. In India, however, though there are oil wells in Assam and at Attock, the supply is negligible, so small that it need not enter into our calculations. It should, however, be remembered that no intensive survey of the mineral oil resources of India have yet been made. Intensive exploration of sub-oil wealth has been neglected in the past and may yield unexpected results in the future. But at the present time India's fuel supply is dependent on Burma and Persia. Unless these interests are safeguarded, the whole position of India will be seriously jeopardised.

The necessity for close association of Burma with the defence system of India is all the more emphasised by this fact. Also for the same reason it becomes a major interest of India to see that both Iraq and Persia remain free and independent and do not fall within the orbit of potentially hostile powers.

It is obvious from what has been stated that the Indian Ocean will be one of the major problems of the future. The security she has enjoyed for over 150 years (from 1784 to 1941) has been completely shattered by the events of the last few years. With major powers developing so near the area, the old conception of that ocean as a preserve has to be given up. America, China and perhaps Russia will have access to the sea, in a manner totally different from what the European nations had in the centuries that followed Vasco da Gama's arrival. Then the nations of Europe alone counted on the sea. If the Atlantic was mastered, Indian Ocean went along with it. Further, the conditions of sailing in the eighteenth century made only one route (*i.e.* via Good Hope) practicable. When the steam ship was discovered, Great Britain was the unchallenged mistress of the seas and was already in possession of the vital areas that controlled navigation. Today the Pacific is as important as the Atlantic. Great Britain, by the mere fact of her distance is at a great disadvantage here in comparison with countries directly bordering the Pacific.

As we have come to know by painful experience the Indian Ocean can be attacked from the Pacific, if Singapore is mastered. Even if Singapore is impregnable and is held and secured, the challenge may come through the Straits of Sunda. Such a challenge from a first-class naval power cannot be met effectively by a navy whose main strength must always be devoted to the defence of Britain's European interests. It follows as a matter of course that only on the basis of a regional organisation of which India will be the secure and firm foundation can the safety of the Indian Ocean be assured.

Such a regional organisation, if it is to secure the safety and freedom of the Indian Ocean, must consist of representatives of Britain, India, South Africa and Australia, for all these have vital interests on the Indian Ocean. It is not a matter for India alone, though it is primarily her interests that have to be safeguarded, and it is she who stands to suffer most by a hostile domination of the Indian Ocean. By her strategic position and as a result of her vulnerability, the problem becomes one of paramount importance to her and any scheme of Oceanic defence has to be based on her.

The conversion of India into an industrially strong country is essential for a scheme of regionalism. Her industry must be self-sufficient and not dependent on machinery imported from other countries. She must be in a position not only to build her own ships, but to equip them on the most up-to-date lines. The heavy industries on which alone a naval power can exist must be built up in India. The problem is not exclusively one of peninsular India. Ceylon and Burma are equally interested and hence the political organisation of the Indian Empire should be broadened so as to include these two countries for defence purposes. The triune commonwealth envisaged in my book " The Future of South East Asia " is therefore, an essential pre-requisite for any scheme of regional organisation, which will be in a position to undertake the defence of the Indian Ocean.

However strongly organised on the main land, the defence of the long and open Indian coast line, not to speak of the active control of the Ocean, is possible only by having suitable island cover as advanced bases. The possession of the Andamans and Nicobars gives protection to the East coast and secures adequate control of the Bay of Bengal. Without Aden and Socotra the defence of the Arabian sea is impossible and the island of Mauritius is clearly indicated as the outpost in the south. With a ring of fortifications covering these islands the coast line of India can be protected for the future and the lines of communications on the sea vital to Indian interests secured firmly.

An exclusively land policy of defence for India will in future be nothing short of blindness. No other policy was required in the past, as the Indian Ocean was a protected sea—a British lake. The mere existance of the Grand Fleet was sufficient to secure the safety of India. But today the position is different. The freedom of India will hardly be worth a day's purchase, if Indian interests in the Indian Ocean are not to be defended from India, especially, as in the changed circumstances analysed above, the British fleet will be in no position to maintain that unchallenged supremacy which it possessed for 150 years. The defence of India's shores cannot be left any longer to the British navy.

This summary survey of Indian Ocean problems from the earliest times has, I hope, clearly proved that till at least the arrival of the Portuguese at the end of the fifteenth century, Indian interests were preponderant in the Indian Ocean.

Indian ships for most of that time, *i.e.* till the beginning of the fourteenth century had the lions' share of traffic, while the Arabs and the Chinese freely participated in the trade. Trade with India constituted from the beginning of navigation the main cargo of the innumerable vessels that plied the Indian Ocean. Though after the battle of Diu, the mastery of the sea passed from Indian hands, India's importance in the Oceanic area did not in any way diminish as a result. On the other hand, it can be said that it is her position on the Indian continent that gave to Britain her undisputed mastery in the Ocean and made it possible for her to extend her dominion to the Pacific.

The commercial interests of India, though they have changed their character have also increased during the last century and a half. Her vast markets and her great natural resources can be reached only though the Indian Ocean and her recent industrial growth, with consequent expansion of trade emphasises the necessity of safe sea communications. Also her interests in the Indian Ocean, based as they are on the inescapable facts of geography, have become more important than ever before.

A direct responsibility now rests on India to face these problems. India aspires to be a free nation and Great Britain has recognised her claim to national independence, whether it be within the framework of the British Empire or otherwise. But no kind of freedom for India is possible unless she undertakes the responsiblity of her own defence and that, we have proved, is predominantly an Oceanic problem. Unless India is prepared to stand forth and shoulder the responsibility of peace and security in the Indian Ocean, her freedom will mean but little. She will be at the mercy of any power which has the command of the sea, as it will be impossible for us to require of Britain to hold the Indian Ocean indefinitely in our interests when we deny her interests in India.

Only in co-operation with Britain is Oceanic defence based on India possible in the circumstances of today, when those who are in a position to make a bid for its mastery are among the greatest naval powers of the world. It would be ridiculous in the extreme for India to pretend that within the course of at least another half a century, an Indian navy, however well organised, will be in a position to stand up to a major naval power like America or Japan. The control of the Indian Ocean, must, therefore, be a co-operative effort of India and Britain and other Commonwealth units having interests on the Ocean with the primary responsibility lying on the Indian Navy to guard the steel ring created by Singapore, Ceylon, Mauritius and Socotra. With the naval might of Britain in the background and with the whole policy of the Commonwealth decided by a Supreme Council enabling the total power of the Empire to be brought to bear at any threatened point, such a defence of India will not be outside the range of practicability.

It is demonstrably clear that the future of India depends on the evolution of an Oceanic policy, and on a political organisation that can shoulder the responsibility and has necessary geographical advantages. Such a policy has already been sketched in its bare outlines. The political organisation essential for its effective implementation cannot be discussed here, but may be summarily stated as involving two factors. The first is the external organisation of India as an independent and free unit of the Commonwealth. The outlines of such a proposal will be found in the Appendix entitled "Imperial Organisation." The second is the internal organisation of India on a firm and stable basis in association with Burma and Ceylon.

These two are the essential pre-requisites to a realistic policy of Indian defence. Without them it is impossible for India to maintain her position in the Indian Ocean and all ideas of Indian freedom will remain but vague dreams, unless the Oceanic problem is faced frankly and solved satisfactorily.

Appendix I.

IMPERIAL REORGANIZATION.

What dominates all discussion of Imperial Reorganization is the geographical distribution of the Empire. Unlike all previous Empires (with the exception perhaps of Spain) the British Empire is neither continuous in territory nor compact in organization. The Empires of the past had geographically expanded over neighbouring territories, as is the case today with the Soviets, or with the Republic of China. It is only the maritime Empires of Spain and France that had similar hemispheric problems, but their historical evolution from the point of view of both their colonies and their Imperial possessions did not give rise to problems of organization similar to those which face the British Commonwealth today. Algiers which is the only colonial area with a settled French population is a part of metropolitan France. So far as other areas are concerned, they are governed directly from France and the question of the adjustment of their relations with the mother country on the basis of local freedom has not arisen. The case of the British Empire is very different. The Dominions are recognised as Sovereign States and are united to the mother country only by a common loyalty to the King and by a like-mindedness in political ideas. So far as India is concerned, her position, though still undefined, is in the process of rapid evolution towards the same goal. Whatever be the form of her future constitution, the basic assumption is that her association with the rest of the Empire will also be voluntary and governed by the same principles and considerations as in the case of the other Dominions.

If organisationally no other Empire had to deal with a similar problem, geographically also the position is unique. Great Britain has not only interests in all the continents, but she is *a great power in each one of them.* Spain no doubt had exclusive power for a long time in America; Russia has wide and dominant interests both in Asia and in Europe. The U.S.A. strides the western Hemisphere, but Britain alone is a great power in everv continent. She shares the hegemony of

Africa with France; in Asia there are the other great powers of Japan and Russia to reckon with; Australasia is Britain's exclusive interest and though there is no rivalry for power in America, Britain by her position in Canada and her interests in Argentine shares with the U.S.A. the mastery of the New World. Thus everywhere Britain has to maintain her position as a world power.

The control of the strategic areas also reflects this position. With Gibraltar and the Suez Canal safely in British hands, and with Malta and Cyprus and with growing interests in Palestine, the Mediterranean continues to be what it has been since the treaty of Utrecht, an essentially British sea. With her authority in India and with the flanks fully guarded by Singapore and South Africa, the vital expanse of the Indian Ocean was a British lake from the time of the withdrawal of the French fleet under Baille de Suffren in 1773 to the occupation of Singapore by the Japanese. Though the mastery of the Pacific was shared with Japan and U.S.A., there was no question of Britain's own authority in the areas that concerned her. Thus except for limited areas, like the Baltic, the Black Sea and the North China Sea, the Empire had not merely interests to safeguard but to maintain her position as a great power, if her organization and structure were to be secure.

Britain's land interests have not received the consideration they merit. While it is generally true that it was by her command of the seas that she was able to maintain her position in the past, and will to a large extent in the future, it is clear that the position has considerably changed in this respect, especially in relation to India and the Middle East. The growth of importance in Imperial policy of the area between the Levant and India is a fact which is only now gaining appreciation. The land defence of the Indian Empire (including in this phrase Burma also) has revealed new and significant problems. As Britain's postion in the Indian Ocean is dependent primarily on India the questions that arise in regard to the Middle East region and the defence of the Eastern boundaries of Burma have an Imperial significance which has to be taken into account.

The necessity for a reorganization of the Imperial machinery has been demonstrated by the events of the last few years.

The present machinery for the co-ordination of Imperial policies consists in the main of:—

(a) direct communication with Dominion Governments;
(b) continuous discussions with High Commissioners;
(c) periodical meetings of Imperial Conferences; and
(d) the Committee of Imperial Defence.

This organization apart from being nebulous has revealed great weakness in the following respects.

The Dominions have the right of direct representation in foreign countries and this right has been exercised by those Governments by appointing Ministers to States in which they have considerable political or economic interests, e.g. Canada in U.S.A. and France. The procedure in force where such separate representation exists may be summarised as follows:—

(a) Other units of the Commonwealth should be kept informed of any negotiations and given an opportunity to express their views; and
(b) None of His Majesty's Governments can take steps which might involve the other governments of His Majesty in any active obligations without their definite assent.

How seriously this second principle restricts the initiative and renders the voice of Britain ineffective in times of crisis can be imagined. Under the present procedure Great Britain cannot enter into definite and binding commitments, except in regard to the United Kingdom and territories directly under her authority, without the consent of each Dominion. The geographical distribution of the Empire renders it impossible for each unit to feel the same interest in affairs arising in a particular part of the world which may affect the Empire as a whole.

The procedure of direct consultation and consent in matters of foreign policy would therefore lead either to indecision and lack of initiative, or to the assumption of both by the Government in the United Kingdom. The utmost that will be possible at a crisis will be to keep the Dominion Governments informed. So long as Britain's foreign policy is mainly European in its outlook this may not lead to any serious difficulties, though it is obvious that the people, say of Australia, could not feel a life and death interest in the future of the smaller States of Europe. But *ex-hypothesi* Britain's position requires a foreign policy in which every part of the world is equally important and it is inconceivable that if decisions are to be taken in respect of the Islamic East, or in respect of policy to be pursued towards China, both of which will become tremendously important in the immediate future, such decisions could be taken without previous consultation and discussion with a free India. Again the Pacific policy of the Empire will be as much a concern of Australia and Canada as of Britain. In matters of foreign policy the Empire can no longer be satisfied with the machinery now in existence.

War is the ultimate sanction of all policy and though the word "Defence" may be preferred as being less aggressive, there is no doubt that what we have to consider is not merely the question of defending the territorial integrity of the Empire when attacked, but of enforcing by war if necessary the policies considered essential for the safety of the Empire. From this point of view the "Defence" of the Empire has to be reckoned as being indivisible. The establishment of the Committee of Imperial Defence recognized this principle, but its weakness came from the fact that it was principally consultative and did not function as an Imperial General Staff. It is fully recognised that the democratic character of the Government of Britain and the Dominions render an Imperial General Staff in its proper sense impossible, if, as is necessary, it has to be autonomous and work in extreme secrecy and entirely unconcerned with shifting political conditions. An organization of the kind that has been functioning in Germany and Japan would make Parliamentary Government nugatory. Nor can it be reconciled with the sovereignty of the Dominions and the freedom of India.

The above analysis leads us to the formulation of the nature of the problems to be solved if an over-all Imperial machinery is devised. They may be stated as follows: Whatever Imperial machinery is devised must ensure :—

(i) the freedom of the units, Great Britain, the Dominions and India;

(ii) the maintenance of the democratic structure of the different Empire Governments;

(iii) without prejudice to either of the above principles,

secure unity of purpose in the High Policy of the Empire, to prevent indecision at critical moments and ensure firm action when required; and

(iv) to devise and co-ordinate continuously all measures military, economic, scientific, financial and political for giving effect to the policies decided upon.

If these are recognised to be the requirements of the over-all organization to be created after the war, then it is obvious that they have to take the form of a Supreme Council, whether Federal or plenipotentiary and an executive organization for Defence, whether an Imperial General Staff, or merely a reconstituted Committee of Imperial Defence.

APPENDIX II.

REGIONAL ORGANISATIONS.

One of the main developments of the interlude between the two wars, whose permanent importance to the Empire has only now been brought home, is the growth of regional problems outside Europe which have a vital bearing on world strategy. In the eighteenth century the control of the Mediterranean was sufficient to ensure an effective and in most cases decisive voice in European policy. In the nineteenth century other regions had also grown in importance, but it was still possible, especially after the construction of the Suez Canal, to control events in the Middle East and the Indian Ocean through that sea. The Far East did not count as a problem in world politics.

In the period that followed the Great War the importance of the new regions was concealed by certain facts. The Indian Ocean remained to all outside appearance a British lake, with its eastern door securely locked by the port of Singapore and its lines of communications commanded from India and South Africa. The Pacific Ocean outside Japanese home waters seemed secure from the British point of view. With an advance base at Hong Kong and the lines of communication safeguarded by the Philippines, the Hawaii Islands and the naval bases in the south, there seemed to be no possibility of a Japanese threat to this area. The Australian region was considered to be outside any zone of foreign influence. Similarly though the Middle East assumed a new importance and land power acquired a new significance with the Russian border extending from Armenia to the Pamirs, the precarious balance of forces in the Far East enabled the amphibious power of Britain in Asia, to overlook its immediate implications.

The present war has clearly shown that regional problems have to be studied with reference to the forces operating in those areas. The happenings in Malaya and Burma and the ease with which Japan conquered the East Indies and threatened the security of The Indian Ocean have demonstrated that, however much the authorities responsible for Imperial Defence may have been ready with plans to meet German aggression against Austria or Poland, the pressure of public opinion had led them to relegate to a secondary place the strategic problems of the new regions which had gained steadily in military and naval importance.

This weakness was inherent in the policy of the Empire, which having a world-wide Dominion to defend considered itself in its foreign policy a purely European power. The tradition of William III, Pitt and Palmerston dominated not merely the Foreign Office but it would seem the Committee of Imperial Defence.

If this mistake is not to be repeated it is obvious that there should be a clear appreciation of regional interests and a close co-ordination of Imperial policy in terms both of the Centre and the periphery. The different regions of the Empire which have their own special problems should receive full consideration in the determination of Imperial policies. Taking Asia as an example, it is clear that the problems of the Indian Ocean have to be studied with special reference to the interests of India, Australia and Africa and Britain's own interests in the lines of maritime and air communications.

Similarly the problems of the Middle East have to be studied from different aspects. The South China Sea is another area which will grow in importance, even if it is assumed that Japan will cease to be a first-class naval power. If a Central Council of Defence is to be responsible for the problems of Defence of all these, it is impossible to see how these outlying areas will receive the attention due to them. The only possibility is to have regional Councils of Defence.

A Council of Asia based on India, a Council of the Pacific based on Australia, a Council of the Middle East based on Palestine, in which apart from Britain, the Empire countries will be represented both politically and by an economic and service staff may be able to undertake this work. The necessity of political representation does not require to be emphasised. War is too serious a matter, as Clemenceau remarked, to be left to the Generals. The regional Councils should be under a Minister of State of eminence. The choice, it need hardly be said, should not be limited to the ranks of British politicians, but should be from the country immediately concerned. The service chiefs should not merely have experience of the areas which are under the Council, but special qualifications for the posts they hold. The suggestion that there should be an economic staff attached may require explanation.

Nothing has been more clearly established by the events of the last four years than the fact that in these days of total warfare, industrial strength and potential are the most decisive factors. For one thing a modern army (including in it the other arms) is so highly mechanised that only a fully industralised nation can maintain it. The difficulties which India has experienced from the lack of industrial strength in maintaining a modern army would clearly demonstrate that haphazard industrialisation without the necessary scientific basis will not be enough for the purposes of warfare. The economic requirements of Defence have to be continuously studied. The scientific research necessary to create the strength where needed cannot also be neglected. The regional resources have to be explored, exploited and co-related to defence purposes. The conservation of vital minerals and the development of raw materials essential for prolonged warfare and other aspects of peace-time industrial preparation cannot be left to the haphazard action of political groups.

In short the regional councils should have as their object the military and economic self-sufficiency of each region, and must have the necessary freedom and authority.

The Central Organisation in London will reflect all these aspects. Its main function will be to co-ordinate regional activities, exercise supervision over them and above all to lay down the general policies affecting the entire Commonwealth. Its organisation is not easy. In order to be effective and to avoid the weakness which beset the Imperial Conferences and the Committee of Imperial Defence, it has to reconcile the principle of the independence of the units with a measure of control from the centre. For one reason or another the scheme of an Empire Federation is ruled out. But clearly the principle of a co-ordinated policy at the centre and freedom for the units can be reconciled only by the acceptance of a limitation of national sovereignity of the units and an over-riding authority in certain specified matters vested in an organisation created by the units themselves—a sort of Council of the Empire. The difference between a federation and such a body will be that while a federation will have to be vested with executive authority in its own sphere, however limited, the Council of the Empire will have no such functions.

This Council will in essence be a permanent Council of Prime Ministers, working no doubt through Resident Deputies. It is essential that the members of the Supreme Council should be Prime Ministers and not ministers or representatives selected *ad hoc.* The pre-war difficulties of distance and time having been overcome by the development of air transport, there is nothing impossible in arranging for the Supreme Council to hold its primary sessions every quarter, while the day-to-day functions will be carried on by permanent deputies who will themselves be of Ministerial rank.

This Council of the Empire will be the Supreme body and its decisions in matters relating to defence will be binding on the units. Under the Council will be an Imperial General Staff, and an Economic General Staff with permanent secretaries attached to them. The co-ordination of the technical work of the Reginal Councils, the responsibility for seeing that Councils do not follow mutually contradictory policies, and the filling up of gaps from the over-all point of view should be the functions of the two General Staffs.

Parallel with the Supreme Council or the Council of the Empire should be an Imperial Tribunal to hear and decide issues that arise between the units of Commonwealth. The necessity of such a tribunal has long been felt. It came up for discussion at more than one session of the Imperial Conference.

It is obvious that as between the units (including the United Kingdom) controversies often arise which lead to certain acerbity of feeling. The laws of the units regarding naturalisation for instance may conflict, thereby creating confusion. Retaliatory measures may be adopted by one unit against another or trade policy may be pursued by one Dominion which may give legitimate cause for complaint to another. These are only illustrative. Where the issues are justifiable it is obviously more suitable that they should be referred to a tribunal which would be in a position to bring an independent, detached and tempered mind to the solution of such problems.

Such a tribunal for Imperial purposes exists in the Judicial Committee of the Privy Council; but that Committee has jurisdiction only where legal rights are concerned. Further, it cannot deal with issues which arise between States and such issues will have ex-hypothesi a political aspect.

This point was fully appreciated and Lord Sankey's Inter-Imperial Relations Committee in 1930 is understood to have suggested that an Imperial Tribunal should be created *ad hoc* from standing panels nominated by the units or as a premanent body to determine disputes and differences between the units of the Empire. The report of the Committee was considered in the Conference of 1930, which came to the conclusion that the composition of the tribunal should be *ad hoc*, that the competence of the tribunal should be limited to differences between Governments and that the proceedings should be voluntary, not obligatory. The decision to limit the proceedings to *ad hoc* arbitration and to make the reference to the tribunal voluntary left the question unsettled because *ad hoc* arbitration on a voluntary basis is open to any two parties and has long been in use in international relationships. What is required is an obligatory reference to a tribunal, either *ad hoc* or permanent where disputes and differences arise between the members of the Commonwealth. This seems to be a logical corollary to the absence of any right of private war between the units of the Empire. Where the remedy of force is not available, it has to be replaced by law, if the diplomatic courses open to a complaining State fails. Assuming that a Dominion expropriates the property of all nationals of the United Kingdom, pressure no doubt can be exercised through diplomatic channels. If unfortunately no agreement could be reached through that procedure, the complaining government will have no course open, but to exercise sanctions. To do so between the members of the same Commonwealth would be carrying things to a ridiculous point. The only alternative would be a compulsory reference to a Court of Arbitration.

Whether such a Court should be permanently established or selected from a panel is a matter on which there is likely to be differences of opinion. The discussions at previous Imperial Conferences have disclosed a partiality towards *ad hoc* tribunals, as safeguarding the cherished sovereignty of the units. A permanent tribunal would no doubt have many advantages, especially of continuity and tradition which in themselves would be highly valuable. Nor could such a permanent Court be considered as affecting the sovereign rights or status of the independent units of the Dominion. The permanent Court of Justice at the Hague in spite of its weaknesses has shown that such a Court can be established and can function smoothly even as between States which are not tied to each other by any other bonds than that of being members of a comity of nations.

There is, however, no serious objection to the tribunal being selected *ad hoc* from standing panels, so long as reference to the tribunal is obligatory if one of the parties find that no other solution of the dispute is possible. The obligatory character of the tribunal will itself tend to smooth disputes and differences, as the mere fact that the parties have the option of referring the matter to an impartial tribunal will have an immense moral effect. Further, where democratic governments are forced by transient popular opinion, excited by some unimportant event to take measures against another member of the Empire community, the existance of such measures will help to steady opinion and strengthen the hands of the more reasonable elements.

The inter-Imperial Tribunal which is visualised as a co-ordinate institution to the Supreme Political Council should therefore be a permanent body, constituted either out of permanent panels or judges appointed on a permanent basis, to which reference should be as of right.

The Imperial machinery which is envisaged in the present scheme may be diagrammatically shown as follows:—

GOVERNMENTS OF THE INDEPENDENT UNITS OF THE EMPIRE.

Canada, Eire, with U.K.	*South Africa*	*U.K., India*	*Australia—New Zealand with U.K.*
Council of Europe (including America)	Regional Council of the Indian Ocean.	Council of the Middle East.	Regional Pacific Council.

Supreme Council of the Empire.

General Staff	Economic Staff	Political Secretariat	Empire

Such a scheme is no doubt open to many objections. The most important of these may be discussed here. In the first place it will be argued, that a scheme such as has been adumbrated will limit the national sovereignty of the Units and will therefore be a retrograde step. This is an argument which applies to any scheme of Imperial Organization, for obviously, a binding organization will involve some limitation on the authority of the Units. If the constituent parts of the Commonwealth are to hold firmly to the principles of absolute independence, and are to stress again after the war the spirit of over-riding nationalism, then no Imperial Organization of any kind, beyond nebulous schemes for consultation and discussion will be possible.

The events of the last quarter of a century have shown that such a policy is not only short-sighted but fraught with the gravest danger to the Empire. When other nations are integrating into greater Units and their national and human resources are being organised on a planned basis, it will be nothing less than an abdication of the Commonwealth's position in the world to pursue its policy of weakening itself in relation to other Great Powers by lack of a co-ordinated policy and an an adequate development of its strength. The outlines of the world which will emerge after this war, which are becoming sufficiently clear now should make us realise that a predominance based on balance of powers among nations is no longer possible. If the Commonwealth is to speak in the councils of the world in terms of equality with the Soviet and the U.S.A., it will have to be not on the basis of a power weakened at the Centre by indecision, and by a machinery incapable by its very nature of quick decision or initiative, but by a power which has a unity of policy and organized strength. Local nationalisms, and the freedom of individual Dominions in their internal policy are indeed important and have to be maintained, but equally, if we are not to confine ourselves to negative terms, we have to limit them to the minimum extent necessary, to ensure safety and strength to the whole.

A second objection will be that the Organization contemplated is meant more in rivalry with other great States and has as its object the increase in the fighting potential of the Empire; that, however, camouflaged by a political superstructure, in essence it is the creation of an Imperial General Staff which will not only undermine the liberties of the democratic Units but by its very nature be a threat to the peace of the world. A State organized on a war basis, it has been well said, must always be tempted to take full advantage of that Organization and it may be argued that any scheme of Imperial Reorganization such as is contemplated by us, whose object is to make the Commonwealth stronger in relation to other nations, will radically alter the character of the Empire as an Organization for Peace and convert it into an organization for war.

These objections are important and have to be considered in detail.

The first part of the criticism that the Organization suggested will be a military integration in effect is not fair. The military organization while no doubt strengthened and put on a sound basis will be wholly under the Political Council, the Supreme Council of the Empire, which will be a purely civilian body. The paramountcy of civil policy will be safeguarded by the composition of the Council, which will consist of the Prime Ministers of the different Units. The authority of the different Parliaments will function through their accredited leaders, the Prime Ministers, and will remain supreme in all decisions of policy. The general staff will merely carry out the policies so decided and will in no sense be the political power that it is in totalitarian States as it will be subordinate to civilian authorities and will be excluded from any voice in the shaping of policies. The apprehension of concealed Militarism is therefore unfounded.

The fear that the increase in the power of the services and the association of economic and scientific work with regional Councils and the Central Council may lead to a change from a pacific to a war-like attitude cannot be wholly discounted. That is a psychological factor which has to be guarded against by a proper emphasis on the democratic traditions of the Commonwealth. They can be further strengthened by the permanent Civil Secretariat of the Supreme and Regional Councils being constituted entirely from among the senior members of the Civil Services of the Units who working under a parliamentary system will be fully imbued with democratic and non-military traditions.

In brief, the essential issue that has to be faced and solved is whether the present fluid nature of inter-Imperial Organization can be allowed to continue; whether it is in the interests of the Units, the Commonwealth or of the world as a whole ? No two answers are possible to this question. A greater degree of Unity both in policy and in execution is necessary if the

Commonwealth is to survive and have its due share of influence in the world. If this is accepted then it follows that the present emphasis on the unrestricted freedom of the Units will have to be modified. The strength or weakness of any proposals of reorganization must be determined by testing how far it safeguards successfully the rights of the Units while establishing an over-all machinery which will be both practical and effective.

THE END.

GEORGE ALLEN & UNWIN LTD
LONDON: 40 MUSEUM STREET, W.C.1
CAPE TOWN: 58-60 LONG STREET
TORONTO: 91 WELLINGTON STREET WEST
BOMBAY: 15 GRAHAM ROAD, BALLARD ESTATE
WELLINGTON, N.Z.: 8 KINGS CRESCENT, LOWER HUTT
SYDNEY, N.S.W.: BRADBURY HOUSE, 55 YORK STREET

ORMUS

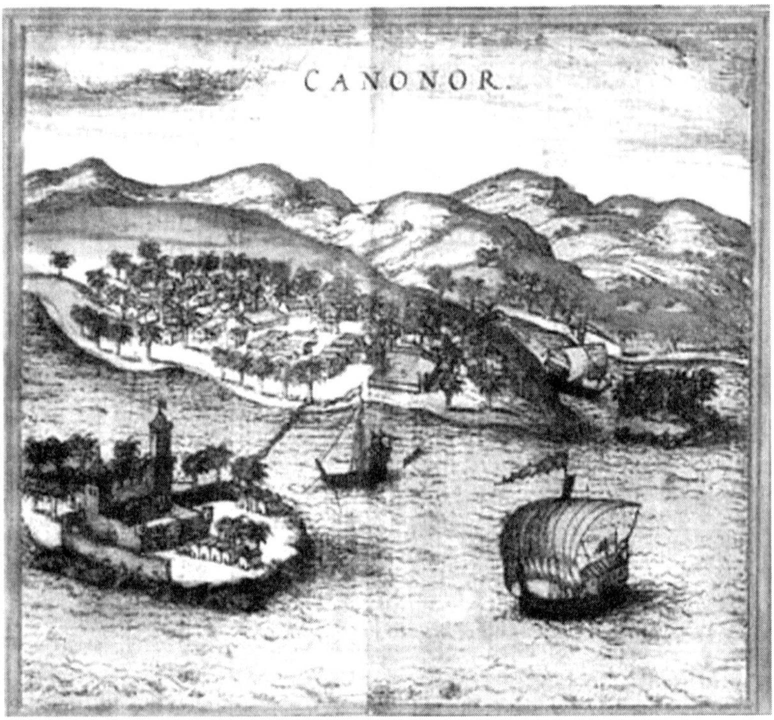

CANONOR

AFOSO DALBOQVERQVE

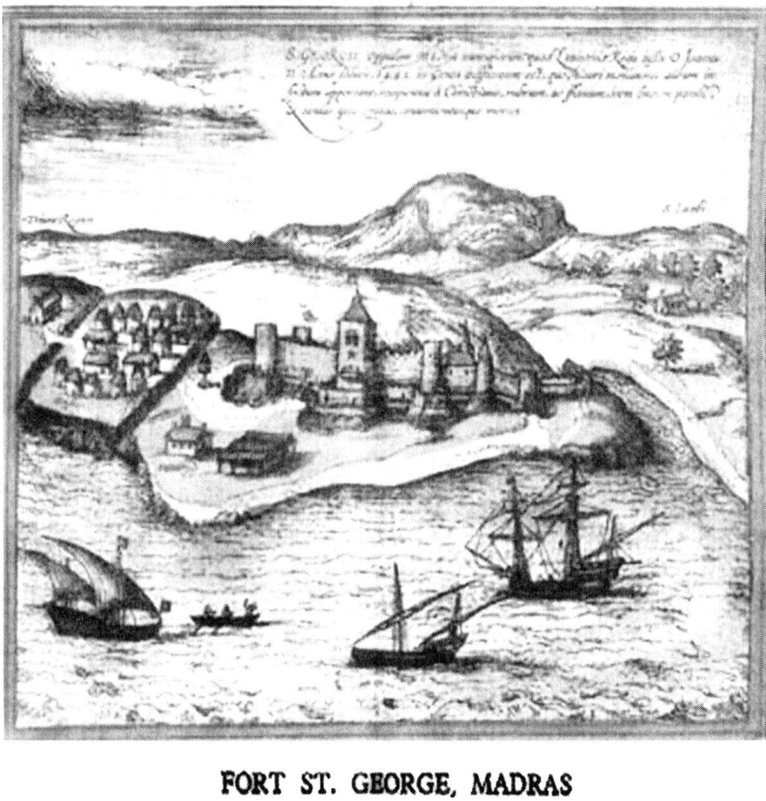

FORT ST. GEORGE, MADRAS

MAHRATTA GRABS AND GALLIVATS ATTACKING AN ENGLISH SHIP. [*Frontispiece.*

(*From a picture in the possession of Sir Ernest Robinson.*)

CALICUT